ONE FAMILY

Before and During the Holocaust

Andrew Kolin

University Press of America, ® Inc.
Lanham • New York • Oxford

Copyright © 2000 by
University Press of America,® Inc.
4720 Boston Way
Lanham, Maryland 20706

12 Hid's Copse Rd.
Cumnor Hill, Oxford OX2 9JJ

Library of Congress Cataloging-in-Publication Data

Kolin, Andrew.
One family : before and during the Holocaust / Andrew Kolin.
p. cm.
Includes bibliographical references and index.
1. Kolniczanski family. 2. Jews—Poland—Genealogy. 3. Holocaust, Jewish
(1939-1945)—Poland. 4. Holocaust, Jewish (1939-1945)—France. I. Title.
DS135.P63 K5655 2000   943.8004'924'0099—dc21   00-023481 CIP

ISBN 0-7618-1678-X (cloth: alk. ppr)

∞™ The paper used in this publication meets the minimum
requirements of American National Standard for Information
Sciences—Permanence of Paper for Printed Library Materials,
ANSI Z39.48—1984

Table of Contents

Acknowledgements

I wish to express my profound gratitude to those persons who provided inspiration, testimony, documents, photographs and research assistance, which made this book possible.

In the United States: I owe both my motivation and a special debt to my mother, Helene Kolin. Over the course of many years, there were many talks about family members prior to, and during, the Holocaust. She took a great interest in the book and and we spoke at length as the project developed. Above all, she made me understand the relationship between history and memory. From my father, Morris Kolin, many important facts were learned about his parents, such as how they lived in Warsaw, their emigration and their life in New York. My aunt, Bella Galanty, was most helpful in piecing together the family puzzle. Without hesitation, she was generous with her time speaking at length about her parents. Aunt Celia Russell was kind enough to discuss her parent's emigration and share numerous documents. My wife, Ellen (Goldbaum) Kolin, gave her time, editorial skills, enthusiasm and careful attention to many tedious technical skills. Assistance by Jean Dickson, curator of the University at Buffalo's Polish Collection is sincerely appreciated. Thanks also goes to Rebecca Farnham for her careful design of the book.

In France: First and foremost, invaluable insights and understanding of family members was due to the generous assistance of my aunt, Mina Kolnitchanski. She maintained an enthusiastic interest in the research and contributed many important photographs and documents. Thanks to another aunt, Marthe Weisberg, of the Centre de Documentation Juive Contemporaire, I had quick access to documents and on short notice, a meeting with Serge Klarsfeld. His kind and generous assistance in obtaining documents on family members is greatly appreciated. Many thanks to Pierre Lautman of the French-Jewish Genealogical Society and to archivist Claude Charlot of the French National Archive.

In Poland: Research assistance was provided by Yale Reisner of the Ronald Lauder Foundation, based at the Jewish Historical Institute. Pawel Dorman and Robert Kozerski also provided assistance.

In Denmark: I am very grateful to Esther and Herman Spilok for the wonderful stories of family members. Arne Knudby researched and translated documents in the Danish Archives.

In Russia: A special thanks is extended to Anton Valdine.

In Sweden: Bertil Wiorek helped me make sense of another branch of the family. Lars Hallberg of the Swedish National Archive was also helpful.

In Israel: Rabbi Bronstein provided research assistance and Nuta Zer-hen provided insights on her ancestors.

And finally, in Australia, I am extremely thankful and grateful to have established and maintained contact with Adam Frydman. His thoughtful insights on the family in Warsaw during the Holocaust were extremely important.

ANDREW KOLIN
ORCHARD PARK, NEW YORK
JANUARY 2000

CHAPTER ONE

Motivations and Methodology

I T WAS A COMBINATION of personal and professional motivations that sparked research on my family's history, prior to, during and after the Holocaust. It is easy to explain my professional motivation in terms of both teaching and researching the Holocaust. My personal motivations, developed from early childhood to adulthood, were the result of numerous conversations with my mother. On relevant occasions, she would relate stories about the family. She combined a very matter-of-fact description with an intensity of feeling. I would listen, never fully understanding the importance of what she told me and yet aware there was so much more to know. When my parents spoke about the family, it was about the families overseas: my father is from Poland, my mother is from France.

The impressions I had of the family were also the result of remarks made by other relatives. From numerous conversations with them, I acquired a striking impression of my relatives, such as how they spoke about the fate of some (not all) relatives during the Holocaust. I recall hearing that one grandfather died in Auschwitz and another emigrated to the United States. One uncle died in Auschwitz, and other uncles died in the Warsaw ghetto. I was told stories about their lives before the Holocaust, about the uncles in Warsaw who were butchers and worked in the slaughterhouse, and how my grandfather fought in World War I. There were numerous stories about emigration to the United States, impressions of

America and the relatives who remained in Europe.

I had one clear idea about the direction in which the research was headed: there would be two primary concerns; a history of my ancestors and what happened to them during the Holocaust.

What was also obvious was that I had no idea what could be learned. I expected that this research would produce three types of results: complete, semi-complete and incomplete material on various relatives.[1] One overriding concern was not to present family members only as Holocaust victims. Instead, emphasis is also placed on them as people, with hopes and accomplishments, and their humanity and how to preserve their memory. In relation to the Holocaust, it means an obligation to speak for the victims, in terms of "circles of care."[2] It is my responsibility as a child of a Holocaust survivor to pay attention to the suffering of the victims and what can be learned about the perpetrators. For all that has been written about the Holocaust, it is, in essence, about the fate of families. By presenting an account of one family, I am avoiding a description of the Holocaust only in terms of documents. Documents are crucial but should be understood in relation to individual accounts, the notion of the Holocaust as what happened to individuals.[3]

In the case of my relatives, integrating testimony with documents produced a coherent chain of events. What happened to relatives is discussed to contribute to a "collected memory,"[4] adding up all the experiences of the victims. Remembering the victims represents a symbolic effort to restore what was taken away, their identities.

The descriptive history of relatives allows for events to speak for themselves and for the speaker to identify with the individuals, with their humanity. The end result is no grand theory about them or about Jews prior to and during the Holocaust. In establishing who they were, their life histories will lead the reader to a very simple and obvious conclusion, that their murder by Nazi perpetrators was, in a word, pointless. The research findings presented are answers to small questions, such as how did they live and cope with hardships and struggle to survive and what was the chain of events leading to their deaths. A historical record serves to undermine the Nazis' efforts to remove all traces of their existence.

From the beginning, three types of sources were utilized, documents, testimony and secondary material. From these sources, gathered over years of research, I was able to construct what I call a preserved memory of my relatives. Derived from these three sources, the memories I assembled of my relatives began to take on different shades of clarity that can be symbolized by images of daylight, dusk and darkness. Where I was able to construct a clear, nearly comprehensive image of specific relatives, including some details on their daily lives, the memories shine as if in daylight. Other stories are punctuated by gaps in information and educated guesses, as if shaded in dusk. There is very little information on relatives in the third category.

I learned to be critical of all sources of information , whether they were documents, personal testimonies or secondary material. Each source had to be weighed in terms of its pluses and minuses. Documents, for example, had much to offer, providing evidence of the perpetrators' actions and the fate of family members. On the minus side, they cannot convey the motivations and day-to-day existence of family members. This is where testimony comes in. It breathes life into documents. It serves to humanize relatives, giving a picture of who they were. Caution should be exercised in relation to testimony. At times, family members can misinterpret events, giving them a meaning they may not have. Secondary material is useful in providing a historical context that shaped the actions of relatives. Overuse of such sources in the narrative, however, can lead to abstractions and overgeneralizations of the effects of events on family members.

I used the sources in combination to create a permanent memory for these relatives, a memory that otherwise would have died along with them. Imperfect as it may be, a preserved memory nonetheless provides surviving family members with their humanity, which the Nazi perpetrators tried to take away from them. It contains two elements: an individual's identity both before and during the Holocaust. In examining the life of family members prior to the Holocaust, a simple question must be answered? Who should be investigated? I decided to narrow the scope of my research to those ancestors of whom I had heard and were closest in their relation to me. I looked first at the origin of the family name, the place where they lived. This allowed me to examine the family from a historical perspective, which allowed me to research such things as the family's probable occupation.

Information on the family's activities before the Holocaust establishes for them a past identity, something the Nazis were dedicated to destroying. This period also allows for an understanding of how the Nazis worked before the Holocaust to systematically dehumanize family members and all Jews by isolating them from the rest of society. The result is a picture of each family member as both individual and victim.

One cannot overstate the value of testimony given by older relatives, without whose contributions the research would quickly have reached an abrupt end. Family research on Polish relatives in the periods before and during the Holocaust presented unique challenges. Most challenging were the attempts to acquire relevant documents. In all but a few cases, I succeeded in obtaining at least some documents on family members. To my surprise, secondary sources also provided important material on relatives, which often was unobtainable from documents.

Throughout the research, I was surprised to discover the diverse range of activities in which relatives were engaged. A complete picture of the colorful, even dangerous, political activities of some family members was obtained from archival papers. Occupational data was obtained from a combination of secondary sources and testimony. Secondary sources were useful throughout the research in providing ethnographic background on areas where the family lived. The combination of archival and secondary sources and testimony drew a complete picture of immigration patterns. All three sources were used to explore the obvious question, Why did some relatives leave Poland while others chose to stay?

In Poland, the massive destruction of so many records during the Holocaust stands out above all others in trying to document the family's experience. I was extremely fortunate to establish regular contact with a survivor who knew the family intimately, which allowed me to learn the fate of many relatives. Secondary sources and a few archival references also were useful in establishing their terrible fate.

As is common on Holocaust research in Poland, there was a lack of information on many relatives. Overall, the research sometimes shed as much light as darkness. One fact was established for certain: the family in Poland was almost completely annihilated by Nazi perpetrators.

By far, the most complete account is of the experiences before and during the Holocaust of relatives who lived in France. My visit to Paris sharply contrasted to a visit on the same trip to Warsaw and clearly demonstrated how place affected my research. I could not help but compare the complete physical destruction of Warsaw during the Holocaust to the preservation of Paris. This difference strongly determined my success in obtaining archival material in Paris. Of equal relevance was the survival of many family members from France. This made the gathering of testimony an easy task, which together with secondary and archival material gave a fairly comprehensive portrait of them. Existing archival and testimonial material on the French side of the family before the Holocaust provided details on their varied activities. Ethnographic material on relevant streets from secondary texts provided clues as to why family members settled in certain locales. Archival files were useful in shedding light on the military and work records of family members. Nonetheless, the documents do not convey the very significant day-to-day effects of those experiences on them. Only the testimony of relatives can give any sense of the thoughts and feelings connected to how these activities are experienced.

This is especially true when documents are unavailable or fragmentary. A case in point was the role of a French relative as the founder of a Landsmanschaft Society in Paris. The few documents that exist were provided by a relative but it was the testimony that gave a sense of its meaning to the family.

Abundant documents and secondary references on the Holocaust in general provided a context of major events in each country, while testimony made it possible to construct a clear memory of how these events impacted on family members. Without this testimony, other sources would have appeared disconnected and incoherent. Through their stories of what happened, relatives and others revealed over and over that the theme of their experiences was survival manifested as flight and resistance. Documents and secondary sources prove their worth over testimony in filling in what testimony cannot provide, a clear picture of the official actions of Nazi perpetrators and how they took steps to dehumanize and eventually exterminate the Jews. The importance of documents was underscored to me when I obtained from the National Archives in France the Aryanization papers on the family business. Unbeknownst to my relatives at the time, the French government in collaboration with Nazi perpetrators, was taking a number of steps, all leading to the seizure of control of the family business. An essential document identified the date when the family's property, including all the furniture in the apartment, was seized.

Documents also were essential in establishing and tracking the movements of relatives caught and detained in transit camps. Other important documents clearly established the terrible end of relatives. Transport lists, camp registration numbers and death notices left no doubt as to their fate. Personal documents and otherwise unofficial documents provided by relatives also were instrumental. For example, I was a given a letter written by a relative interned in a transit camp. Another significant document given by a relative was a series of eyewitness accounts of resistance to the Nazis in her neighborhood distributed by the Communist Party. There was no shortage of secondary accounts on the relevant transports in which relatives were deported to the camps.

In sharp contrast to the experiences of family members in Poland and France were those of relatives who settled in Denmark and the U.S. The obvious and fundamental difference was a simple matter of geography. Denmark's close proximity to Sweden and the United States' physical separation from Europe spared those relatives the terrible fate of their

Polish and French counterparts. Danish relatives have partial memories of persecution and escape but they cannot possess any memory of what it meant to lose loved ones. For American relatives, the Holocaust was distant not only physically, but also as a concept. One can say that relatives who left Poland for Denmark and the U.S. did so unaware that by emigrating, they were ensuring their survival. At the time, their decision to leave Poland was prompted by their desire to escape persecution. This motive does not appear in any immigration documents, only in the testimony of family members. Immigration materials provided the facts on when and where they left, names and dates of birth, but they cannot convey the state of mind of immigrants. Testimony also explains why some relatives chose Denmark and others the U.S. Documents filled in the gaps not covered by testimony such as work histories and how relatives adjusted to life in a new country. Documents and secondary sources were helpful in explaining how Danish relatives adjusted by founding a Landsmanschaft, they also were useful in identifying various occupations of relatives and compensated for unavailable testimony because family members are deceased or are reluctant to express what they remember.

NOTES

[1]This is the case with three relatives known to have survived the Holocaust and who, to this day, have not been located. The three relatives were among those who registered as Polish Jewish survivors under the auspices of the Central Committee of the Jews in Poland from 1945-1947.

Date   25.2.49
Name   KOLNICZANSKI, Hersz   File 18-108
BD   1928   BP   Nat Polish-Jew
Next of Kin   parents:Icek,Sura Book K.II.P.249
Source of Information Central Jew. Committee in Poland,Warsaw
Last kn. Location Legnica Jadwigi 41   Date aft.war-Jan.47

Date   25.2.49
Name   KOLNICZANSKA, Dora   File 18-108
BD   1933   BP   Nat Polish-Jew
Next of Kin   parents: Icek,Sura Book K.II.P.249
Source of Information Central Jew. Committee in Poland,Warsaw
Last kn. Location Legnica Jadwigi 41   Date aft.war-Jan.47

Date   25.2.49
Name   KOLNICZANSKI, Josef   File
BD   1931   BP   Nat
Next of Kin : parents: Icek,Sura Book K.I.I P.249 .
Source of Information Central Jew. Committee in Poland, Warsaw
Last kn. Location Lodz, Wolosanka 76   Date .

Date   25.2.49
Name   KOLNICZANSKI, Icek   File 1
BD   1890   BP   Nat Pol Jew
Next of Kin parents: Mojsze,Chaja Book KIIP249.
Source of Information Central Jew. Committee in Poland Warsaw
Last kn. Location Legnica Jadwigi 41   Date .

The cards indicate that they had fled Poland for Russia. They were repatriated due to three agreements signed in September 1944. For additional details, see the article of Yosek Litvak, "Polish-Jewish Refugees Repatriated from the Soviet Union at the end of the Second World War and Afterwards" in *Jews in Eastern Poland and the U.S.S.R 1939-46* Davies and Polonsky, ed. (St. Martin's Press, New York: 1991)

The final agreement for repatriation was made on July 6, 1945. The Jews who were repatriated from Russia in the years 1944-46 reached a total of 856,127. This is discussed in Lucjan Dobrosyzycki, <u>Survivors of the Holocaust</u> (Sharpe, New York: 1994).

[2]This expression is borrowed from Roger Gottlieb's book <u>Thinking the Unthinkable</u> (New York: Paulist Press,1990), p. 416

[3]Or, as Judith Miller put it, <u>One by One by One</u> (New Haven: Yale Press, 1993)

[4]The larger meaning of how the Holocaust is interpreted. This theme appears in Janes Young, <u>Holocaust Memorials and Meaning</u> (New Haven: Yale Press, 1993)

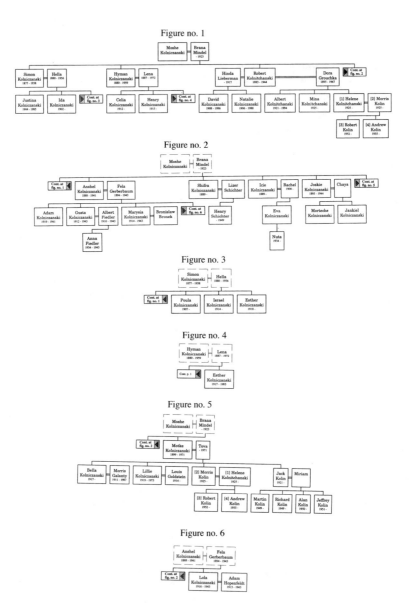

Figure no. 1

Figure no. 2

Figure no. 3

Figure no. 4

Figure no. 5

Figure no. 6

CHAPTER TWO

From Kolnica to Warsaw

T HE RESEARCH BEGINS with a name. Names have a history, as does my last name, Kolin. Testimony from relatives and various documents indicate that Kolin is short for Kolniczanski. The Kolniczanski family was from Poland. The name is a place name, from the village of Kolnica,[5] a small village, six miles south of the district town of Augustow,[6] where the family eventually settled. Kolniczanski means a person from the town of Kolnica. As was the case for many Polish Jews, the Kolniczanski's acquired their name in the early 19th century.

Kolnica is situated close to Kolno Lake, known for its rich supply of fish. The lake is not deep with a maximum of 6 meters in depth with a muddy bottom. The name of the village is derived from this close proximity to the lake. A literal meaning for Kolnica is mud, an obvious reference to the mud in Lake Kolno.

The village was established in an area cleared from forests and by the intiative of the Grodno economic department. The land in that region of Poland was, in the 18th century, under the control of Lithuania with the economic administration of the land based in Grodno. It was a common practice for the king to grant land estates to his followers and trusted servants. In return, they would pay the king an estate tax equal to onefourth of the estate's net annual income. The owners of these estates were given permission to form a village that become known as Kolnica, near cultivated farm land.

The founding of the village and the surrounding grange date back to 1733. In large part, the economic foundation of Kolnica was agriculture. The farming was limited to grains, potatoes, sugar beets and the breeding of cows. For many residents, incomes were supplemented either by working in Augustow or in the fishing industry on Lake Kolno. Some residents produced linen cloth in their homes, which they sold to Jewish traders.

Present-day Kolnica

Little is known of the Jews who lived in Kolnica with the exception of Zawel Berkowicz, who was the first Jew to settle in the village. He was the lessor of an inn in Kolnica. The burghers in Augustow were in competition with Jewish inn lessors. They not only sold drinks to local villagers, they also organized the purchase of goods to be sold in markets and fairs. In 1744, the Burghers of Augustow in an effort to fight against the competition of the inn lessor in Kolnica, Zawel Berkowicz, beat him and destroyed his goods.

The only reference found of a Kolniczanski near Kolnica was an Efraim Kolniczanski, who was responsible for toll charges on a bridge connecting Kolnica and Augustow. Without supporting archival and secondary sources, it was not possible to determine whether or not Zawel

Berkowicz and Efraim Kolniczanski are ancestors. Supporting evidence of a Kolniczanski presence in Augustow was located in the National Archives of Stockholm, Sweden.[7] The name Abram Kolniczanski appears in these documents: he was born in Augustow, Poland in the year 1848. That year is significant in that the Kolniczanski's had lived in Augustow during a period in which the Jewish population in the province grew at a rapid rate: "During the period 1845-1865, Jewish settlement in Augustow province grew about 41%. . ."[8]

As I researched the Kolniczanski's, I wanted to know how to establish with some certainty that Abram Kolniczanski and his relatives were also my relatives. The answer to this question points to the limitations of documents and the importance of testimony from witnesses and relatives. The evidence was provided by Esther Spilok, a Danish relative I had the pleasure of meeting with twice: in Copenhagen and in Paris and with whom I corresponded. Her father was my great-uncle; he had an uncle, Abram Kolniczanski, who migrated to Stockholm from Warsaw. This means that Abram Kolniczanski was the brother of my great-grandfather, Moshe Kolniczanski, who was also the father of Simon Kolniczanski, who will be discussed shortly.

Members of the Wiorek family were kind enough to provide me with a photograph of my great-great-grandfather and his wife.

The lack of archival documents limited the scope of my search for evidence of a Kolniczanski presence in Augustow. Many Jewish records in the Suwalk region were lost or destroyed. The few remaining civil records in the Suwalki archive contain birth and death dates of unrelated Kolniczanski's. Also, until the late 1830's, not all Jewish families living in Augustow had their second names recorded with town authorities. In fact, it was only during the Prussian rule, after 1795, that second names were given to Jewish families. Prior to that, Jews used the names of their fathers as their second names.

My great-great grandparents

The population breakdown in Augustow, as of 1859, showed 3,764[9] Jews or 45.3%[10] of the population. Abram and other members of the Kolniczanski family were, as of 1851, one of "677 Jewish families residing in Augustow and vicinity."[11] The detailed history of the Kolniczanski family begins in Powazki, a small shtetl outside Warsaw. This raises an obvious question: why did the Kolniczanski's emigrate from Augustow to Powazki? There is evidence that large numbers of Jews from the Suwalki province (of which Augustow is a part) left the area, many of whom headed to the United States.[12]

The Kolniczanski's may have migrated from Augustow to Powazki because of the severe famine, which affected Lithuanian Jews and nearby Polish provinces such as Augustow in the years 1867-1869.[13] "A new great famine which fell upon the west Russian provinces in 1868-69 halted the growth and economic progress in Suwalk. Hunger brought many diseases, and some people simply fell in the streets."[14] Other accounts conveyed the chilling details of the famine. "In the streets, synagogues, study halls roam downcast hundreds of people without strength, starving to death. Only their shadows are visible and they only hope for an end to their lives. In schools, children die before their parents' eyes and girls wail in front of their friends."[15] In addition, the famine had a profound economic effect. "Even when the famine subsided, the underlying damage to the city's economy persisted."[16]

It also is possible that something other than the famine was the motive behind the Kolniczanski migration to Powazki. What I do know is that the family moved to Powazki sometime between the years 1848 and 1877. I can make this assumption based on the birth dates of the last Kolniczanski known to have been born in Augustow (Abram, Moshe's brother, born in 1848) and the

Center: Moshe (with beard) and Brana Kolniczanski
Back row, Right: Simon and one of his daughters, Leah, next to him

birth date of the first Kolniczanski known to have been born in Powazki (Simon, 1877).[17]

Moshe and Brana-Mindel[18] are the starting point for the Kolniczanski's of Powazki-Warsaw. They are my great-grandparents. Moshe Kolniczanski was a shoe maker. The evidence appears in the application for citizenship of his first son, Simon who emigrated to Denmark. In the application, he describes himself as "the son of Polish parents, shoe maker Moisov Kolniczanski and his wife, Brana Mindel." He stated that he lived with his parents until he got married in 1899.[19]

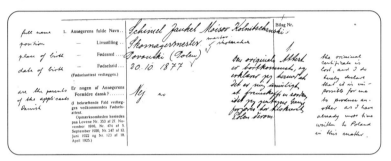

Little is known about Brana-Mindel except that her maiden name was Rothstein and that she died in 1923. This photo, (see next page) taken at her funeral, is the only one obtained of the Kolniczanski's in a group setting with some of the children.

Moshe and Brana-Mindel had eight children: Simon-Jacob (1877), Chaim (1880), Reuven (1883), Anchel (1888), Shifra (1889), Joskie (1895), Icie (1898) and Motke (1899). The Hebrew and diminutive names the parents gave to their children are in many ways a reflection of both the affection and high hopes they had for them. Overall, there was a pattern in the names chosen by the parents, one which can be described as bold, positive and most of all, optimistic. For example, the first child, Simon: the Hebrew reference to the name is "to hear or to be heard."[20] Chaim[21]

Front, L to R: Icie, Chaya, Lola, Bella, Lilly, Jack, Toba
Back, L to R: Shifra, Leizer, Marysia, Adek, Guta, Anchel, Motke, Joskie, Chaya
Center: Fela

and Reuven[22] are defined as meaning life and the joy associated with a son. The names Anchel[23] and Itche[24] mean blessed and laughter. The names Shifra[25] and Mortke[26] are associated with good, beautiful and warrior.

All eight Kolniczanski children married and had children. Since many records were either lost or destroyed prior to and during the German occupation of Poland, complete records of marriages and children's birth dates were established for only four of the eight Kolniczanski's.

There were large gaps in the archives for the civil records as well as tenant records. This fact made the testimony of relatives all the more important.

Simon, the oldest, married Lea (b. 1878) in 1899 at the age of 22, and they had five children: Ida (1901), Justinia (1904), Poula (1907), Israel (1914), Esther (1918). It was Esther (married name is Spilok) who first provided me with the names of Simon's children. Confirmation of the names was acquired through Danish archival sources.[27]

Hyman married Lena (1887) at the age of 30. They were married in Warsaw on December 19, 1910, as indicated on their wedding invitation. They had three children: Celia (1912), Henry (1915) and Esther (1917).

Reuven was married twice, the first time to Hinda (nee Liberman)

INVITATION

With the help of G-d

The year of a good sign and good luck for this couple forever.
We are honored to request your honorable presence to attend and share our
joy and the occasion of the celebration of our children.

The wonderful groom, CHAIM KOLNICHANSKY
With his chosen, the wonderful bride, LEAH FRYD

Which shall take place, G-d willing, with good mazel and at the right and
good time, on Tuesday, in the week of the Torah Reading of Veyeshev
[Genesis 37-40], the 19th of Kislev 5671 [December 19, 1910] in Warsaw, at
the Parizer Maranovska Hall 34.
G-d willing, to the celebration of your children we shall lovingly return
the favor.

In-laws: MOSHE KOLNICHANSKY, father of the groom
    SARAH FRYD, mother of the bride

Ceremony (canopy) at 9.   Party at 10

Telegram address: Warszawa sala Paryzka
Printed by P. Mizna Golevki 15

and then to Dora (nee Grouchka). From Reuven's first marriage, the children were David (1908) and Natalie (1906). From the second marriage, there were three children: Albert in 1921, and the twins, my mother, Helene and her sister Mina, in 1925. From Dora's first marriage, there was a son, Adolph (1914). The detailed material I have is the result of significant contributions from my mother and Aunt Mina. They provided copies of his civil records, which confirm the date of their marriage and the birth dates of their children.[28] They speak of their family with great warmth of feeling and also arrive at a profound understanding of people and events. In many ways, they inspired this research.

Mortke, the youngest of the Kolniczanski brothers, married earliest, at only 17 years of age. His wife, Taube, was the same age. His application for naturalization has the date of his marriage.[29] They had four children, Bella in 1917, Lillie in 1919, Jack in 1921 and my father, Morris in 1925. I am fortunate to have obtained material on my grandfathers, Reuven and Motke because my mother and father are cousins. My mother is the daughter of Reuven, my father is the son of Motke. There are no dates of marriage for Anchel, Joskie, Icie or Shifra.

The fourth Kolniczanski, Anchel, married Fela (born in 1894) and had four children: Guta (1912), Marysia (1914) Lola (1916) and Adam (1919).[30]

Unfortunately, the material gathered on the next three Kolniczanski ancestors is fragmentary. In the case of Icie, he married Rachel, born in 1900 and they had one child, Eva. Eva's daughter, Nuta, with whom I spoke, did provide some information in bits and pieces. Joskie married Chaya and they had two sons, Mortche and Jankiel. Shifra, the only daughter of the Kolniczanski's, married Leizer Schnichter. They had one son, Henry.

It can be established with some degree of certainty that the Kolniczanski family lived and worked in Powazki, which was a separate village until it was incorporated as a suburb of Warsaw in 1916.[31] Powazki would qualify as a typical shtetl. It was referred to as "Jewish Town Powazki."

In the 1880s, "the majority of the 3,000 residents were Jewish."[32] By and large, these were poor families living in little wooden houses. Photographs of Powazki give credence to the notion that the town with its low wooden buildings had an atmosphere of a shanty town. Living conditions in Powazki were far from ideal; prior to its incorporation with Warsaw, the town was "neglected in every respect; largely deprived of sewers, pavement and suitable lighting. . .in a deplorable sanitary condition."[33] In terms of the number of houses and stores, as of 1905, Powazki had "134

Powazki, 1936

houses, 85 stores, a public and a military grinding mill, petroleum warehouse, 4 bakeries, slaughterhouse, forge, pharmacy and school." [34]
In 1912, of the 5,978 residents, 2,325 were Jewish. [35] Powazki remained heavily Jewish into 1939, when 77% of the residents were Jewish. [36]
Eventually, the Kolniczanski's settled in the Zachodnia district, which was a largely Jewish section of Warsaw. They did not settle in the most well-known and heavily Jewish section of Muranow, but in Mirow. There

also were other ethnic and non-Jewish groups living in Zachodnia district.

In the case of Anchel Kolniczanski, confirmation of his family's residence appears in telephone directories for the years 1932 to 1936. [37] Both his residence and business addresses are listed. He had an apartment at 5 Ogrodowa and his butcher shop was on 9 Solna Street [38]. As early as 1920, Anchel had a butcher shop on that street. [39] His store was close to Plac Mirowski and Hale Mirowskie, centers for shops and meat trading. At the time, Solna was one of the

Solna Street, 1915

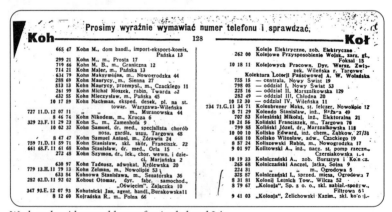

Work and residence addresses for Anchel and Icie

most busy commercial streets in Warsaw, with many little shops, hardware and haberdashery stores.

Both Anchel and my grandfather, Motke, are listed in a 1929 Polish business directory[40] under "Butchers." Icie is listed as living at 7 Ogrodowa under the Polish term Sprzed Miesa, which translates as meat sales. Ad-

```
Polish Business Directory from 1929 (Ksiega Adresowa Polski).
was able to find under "Butchers":

Kolniczanski Anszel, Smolna 9
Kolniczanski M., Namiestnikowska 2
```

ditional information from address books called Businesses for Poland, indicate the businesses of Anchel's daughters Lola and Guta. Guta had a tobacco business at 4 Elektoralna[41]. According to Adam Frydman, "to acquire a tobacco concession in Poland, you had to have influence," a reference to Anchel's influence. Anchel's other daughter, Lola, had a business at 60 Leszno.

The home address of Motke Kolniczanski was 23 Krochmalna Street. "The streets were rough, cobbled and dirty, there were deep gutters and laundry hung from every balcony." [42] Considered to be "one of the poorest, narrowest, dirtiest and most densely populated streets in Warsaw,"[43] Krochmalna was also home to many, seedy, underworld dealings. In my father's words, "when things got better, we moved to Choldna Street," considered at the time to be a more upscale residence.

Notes

[5]The evidence for this claim appears in Alexander Beider, <u>A Dictionary of Polish Surnames from the Kingdom of Poland</u> (NewJersey: Avotaynu, 1996) p. 252.

[6]Beider defines the "anski" as meaning from, or living in, a specific locality. He identifies the source of Jewish surnames as Christian authorities granting special decrees. It was possible to construct a brief history of Kolnica using the following sources: Wojciech Batura, Andrzej, Dzieje Augustowa. od Zalozenia do 1945 <u>Suwalki: Roku</u>, 1977 and Przeglad Augustowski <u>Po Swiateczna Jemioleo, 1996-98</u>, as well as interviews with Wojciech Batura, historian and director of museum in Augustow, as well as with villagers in Kolnica.

[7] National Archives, Stockholm, Sweden. Document No. 61-2697-97

[8]This is elaborated in "The Emigration from Suwalk, excerpt from Jewish Community Book of Suwalk," <u>Landsman</u>, Summer 1990, p. 8

[9]Y. Alexandroni, Y. ed. <u>The Yizkor Book of Augustow and Vicinity</u> (Tel Aviv: Organization of Jews of Augustow and Vicinity, 1966), p. 37

[10]Ibid, p. 40

[11]Ibid

[12]<u>Landsman</u>, Fall 1990, p. 3

[13]Alexandroni, p. 45

[14]Ibid

[15]Ibid

[16]<u>Landsman</u>, Fall 1990, p. 9

[17] It appears that various branches of the Kolniczanski family as a whole moved to Powazki. Supporting evidence appears in the archival documents of Abram Kolniczanski and his children. On the document, Abram's place and date

	Our date	Our reference
	October 1, 1997	61-2697-97

Dear Professor Kolin,

Enclosed you will find copies of two death certificates (dödsbevis), which I got from the City Archives of Stockholm. They were found in the archives of the public health committee of Stockholm (Stockholms stads hälsovårdsnämnd), volumes E II a:723 and 912.

Depåbyrån
Depåområde 2
L. Hallberg

Abram Kolniczanski was a Polish citizen when he died. He was born in Augustow and was a Russian citizen before Poland's independence. Perhaps the Jewish Congregation in Stockholm could have some more information on him.

Sincerely yours,

Lars Hallberg

Our date
August 14, 1997

Our reference
61-2697-97

Depåbyrån
Depåområde 2
L. Hallberg

Dear Professor Kolin,

The archives of the National Board of Aliens (Statens utlänningskommission) and its predecessor Statens polisbyrå are kept in the National Archives. According to the documents there Szyfra (Sifre, Schiffra, Sofia) Kolnitschanski (Kolniczanska, the spelling of the names varies) (born May 30, 1889) immigrated to Sweden in May 1914 (or 1913). She came to Sweden with her father Abram and earned her living partly by, illegally, selling ladies' underwear, for which she was fined in 1927 and 1930. Later on she occasionally worked as a dressmaker. She lived and died in Stockholm, unmarried, on February 25, 1956. I have copied her forms of application for permission to sojourn in Sweden in 1918 and 1924 and for visa in 1927.

Her father Abram Kolniczanski (born March 25, 1848) apparently at first stayed in Sweden for some years. He returned here in September 1921 to stay with his other daughter Sonja Wiorek. He died in Stockholm on July 1, 1934.

Sonja (Sima) Wiorek (born December 22, 1875) and her husband Samuel Abraham Wiorek (born January 1, 1880) immigrated to Sweden in 1913. They died in Stockholm on November 16, 1947 and December 16, 1953, respectively. Their son Isaac Wiorek (born October 10, 1901) became a Swedish citizen in the 1920's.

Other relatives are also mentioned in the documents. In 1925 Sofia's and Sonja's brother Jacob (Jankiel) Kolniczansky (born March 1, 1894) repeatedly applied for permission to come to Sweden to work or to visit his relatives, but this was denied by the Swedish authorities. He then lived in Lübeck. In December 1926 the sisters mentioned that they had a brother in Copenhagen who was dying.

Sincerely yours,

Lars Hallberg

National Archives
TELEPHONE + 46 8 737 63 50
TELEFAX + 46 8 737 64 74

POSTAL ADDRESS
P.O. BOX 12541
S-102 29 STOCKHOLM
SWEDEN

VISITING ADDRESS
FYRVERKARBACKEN 13–17
STOCKHOLM

of birth are listed as Augustow, 1848. His daughter, Shifra, states that her place of birth is Warsaw in the year 1889. His son Joseph and his daughters also migrated to Sweden. He had an apartment with a tailor shop for many years. The Stockholm National Archive provided a summary of Shifra's work history.

Abram Kolniczanski was living in Powazki prior to his immigration to Sweden. A Warsaw police department report discusses a robbery attempt in 1913 at the home of Abram Kolniczanski.

```
      4th departament of the Police Departament.  1913. file 8,
   part 6.

      sheets 134-135.

      The assistant of the Warsawa general-goventor reported to
   the Departament of the police:

         27th of  Sept.,  1913,  about 4 hours in the night to the
   Povonzki house-owner Abram K.,   65 years old, somebody knocked
   to his  flat.  When K.  opened a door,  5 offenders run to his
   flat and,  threating by the revolvers,  demand  to  give  them
   money. K  gave  them  3  rubles,  which  was in his flat.  The
   offenders made a search in his flat, and, find nothing, beat K
   and run  away.  R··
```

[18]I am very thankful for the generous assistance of my aunt, Bella Galanty, a Kolniczanski descendant, the daughter of my grandfather. Bella Galanty was instrumental in describing the numerous Kolniczanski's of Powazki and Warsaw. Her discussions of my grandfather were of equal importance.

Her contribution — and those of other relatives — is all the more important, because my many efforts to obtain from Poland civil and tenant records for family members were unsuccessful. The near-total destruction of records during the Holocaust has made searching for such documentation often impossible. However, such difficulties were prevalent in the pre-Holocaust period as well. In Simon Kolniczanski's application for citizenship in Denmark in 1928, he complains that even after repeated attempts to obtain his own birth certificate from Warsaw authorities, he remained unsuccessful.

Furthermore, his daughter's application for citizenship in Denmark reveals additional difficulties in obtaining or relying on Polish civil records decades before World War II. According to Poula Kolniczanski's application for citizenship, the Polish authorities had her birthdate as September 8, 1907, when in actuality, it was December 10, 1907. Danish genealogist Arne Knudby paraphrased Poula's discussion of the two dates on her citizenship application:

"The applicant cannot explain the two different dates, but as far as she has been told, her birthday is on the 10th of December 1907 and she has always celebrated her birthday on the 10th of December. The father of the applicant, master shoemaker, S.J. M. Kolniczanski, explains that his daughter was born on the 10th of December 1907. Why the Polish authorities have written the 8th of September 1907 on the birth certificate, he does not know. But he explains that when he lived in Poland, there was no obligation of reporting the birth of a daughter to the authorities. As a consequence of this, the birth of a girl was often only reported many years later, and certificates from the authorities were often totally misleading."

[19]Danish National Archives, Copenhagen, Number 1003-27

[20]Alfred Kolatch, Complete Dictionary of English and Hebrew First Names (New York: Jonathon David Publishers, 1984) p. 214

[21]Ibid, p. 52

[22]Ibid, p. 196

[23]Ibid, p. 22

[24]Ibid, p. 120

[25]Ibid, p. 419

[26]Ibid, p. 165

[27]op. cit. Danish National Archives

[28]Their originals came from the Ville de Paris, 11 Arrondissement, Reg. No. 438

[29]U.S. Department of Immigration and Naturalization

[30]It was sheer good fortune to make contact with Adam Frydman. He deposited pages of testimony at Yad Vashem. A two-and-a-half year correspondence began. In one of his letters, he explained why he had such in-depth knowledge of the Kolniczanski family. Adam Frydman's mother had a sister, Fela. She married Anchel Kolniczanski. There were close business contacts between the two families as well. Adam's father was an accountant for the Kolniczanski's in the Praga slaughterhouse.

[31]This is explained in the Atlas of Warsaw's Architecture (Warsaw: Arkady Publishers, 1977) p. 30. Powazki was one of several suburbs incorporated into the city in the spring of 1916.

[32]Slownik Geograficzny Krolestwa Polskiego (Warsaw, 1883) pp. 885-6

[33]Stephen Corrsin, Warsaw Before the First World War (NY: Columbia University Press, 1989, p. 47)

[34]Alexander Janowski, Warszawa, Warsaw: Wydawnictwo Polskie 1966, p. 48

[35]Slownik Geograficzny Krolestwa Polskiego Ibid.

[36]Peter Martyn "The Undefined Town Within a Town," The Jews of Warsaw, ed. Bartoszewski and Polonsky (New York: Oxford Press, 1991) p. 297

[37] Spis Abonentow Warszawskie Siegl Telefonow, Rok, 1931-32

[38] Ibid

[39]"Warszawa" pa 1920 rok, Rok Pierwszy, Pod Redakcja, Tomasza Kozminskiego, p. 613

[40] Ksiega Adresowa Polski, 1929

[41] Spis Abonentow Warszawskie Siegl Telefonow, Rok 1938-39

[42] Isaac Bashevis Singer, Shosha, London: Penguin Books, 1979, p. 68

[43]This description is found in Bernard Goldstein, Twenty Years with the Jewish Labor Bund p. 169

CHAPTER THREE

Political Struggles and Emigration

ROM THE EARLY 1900s until the mid 1930s, members of the Kolniczanski family made choices that divided them into one of two camps: those who stayed and those who emigrated. Out of the eight children of Moshe and Brana Kolniczanski, four left Poland and four stayed. In large part, the collective fate of the Kolniczanski family during the Holocaust depended on that one critical choice.

Reuven Kolniczanski was the first in the family to emigrate. A possible reason for his leaving Poland can be found from two sources, one primary — my mother's statements — and the other secondary. The secondary source is a reference to Reuven: ". . .. he had pulled away from the family traditions. He became a hatmaker and after a certain period, he left for Paris." [44] My mother provided a vivid account of Reuven's manner of thought as a socialist, (he associated with the Jewish Bund) non-religious and cosmopolitan. According to documents obtained from the French department of Immigration and Naturalization, Reuven arrived

Robert Kolnitchanski's application for citizenship

in Paris in October 1902.[45]
There is no doubt as to where
he arrived in France: it was in
Paris, at la Gare de l'Est. For
immigrants from other parts
of Europe, this was their first
point of contact with France.
The immigration docu-
ments contain revealing information about Reuven.
What the documents do not
reveal is that he was a daring
19-year-old who left everyone
he knew, including his large
family, to find himself alone
in Paris.

At the time of this application for citizenship, Reuven
had lived for ten years in Paris
and worked as a pocketbook-
maker. There was no sever-
ance of ties to the

Front Left: Hymie, Front Right, Anchel, Back Center, Reuven

Kolniczanski's still in Poland. This is apparent from a photo taken in 1904
in Paris. A youthful Reuven in the middle is standing; Hyman is in the
front on the left, and Anchel on the right.

Reuven's emigration to Paris in 1902 was part of a larger pattern of
Jewish immigration from Poland. In 1880, a wave of Jewish immigration
began, in large part a response to political repression due to the assassi-
nation of Tsar Alexander II. "By 1900, some 8,000 of them had settled in
Paris."[46] The Jewish population of Paris rose steadily so that as of 1914,
"eastern European immigrants numbered over 20,000, two-fifths of the
Jewish population of Paris."[47]

Reuven's work as a pocketbook worker was consistent with the pattern of work pursued by many eastern European Jewish immigrants. He
was part of what would be called, in the 20s and 30s, small ateliers.

Back in Powazi, his brother Anchel was becoming active in various
political causes. In many ways, he was a fighter. When I interviewed Esther
Spilok in Paris in December 1996, she remembered her father, telling her
of how Anchel fought the Cossacks, when they raided Powazki:

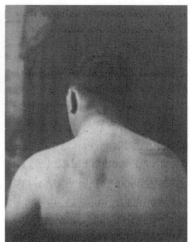

When he knew a pogram was coming, he would go into the
butcher store to get knives and throw them at the Cossacks. They
would chase him. To escape, he would climb to the roof and, jumping from roof to roof, would continue to throw knives at them.
When on some occasions, he was caught, he would be whipped.
He would then go to the public bath, where his wounds were
tended to.

This photo shows Anchel after one of his encounters with the Cossacks.

Esther also spoke of how "at night Anchel would visit my father, who
lived just outside Powazki, to warn them of a raid, when the Cossacks
were coming, so they should flee. Anchel was well-connected with the
police. They would inform him prior to a pogrom."

Secondary sources discuss in detail both the occupational and political activities of the Kolniczanski's in Powazki: ". . . the Kolniczanski's
were meat workers in the Povonzek slaughterhouse."[48]

Meat workers like the Kolniczanski's had to face long hours and ex-
ploitative work conditions:

> The conditions in slaughterhouses are very hard. The work goes
> all day and night and on weekends and holidays, especially in
> butcher's shops. The main problem in our trade are called earn-
> ings. Each journey man wants to have help of as many as possible
> boys, because with the boys it is not necessary to share the earn-
> ings as with another journeyman. So there are many journeymen

without work. Additionally, masters call the journeymen: "hey you" or "do a thing." Butchers! It is time to go on strike and to stop the exploitation. [49]

The Kolniczanski's, especially Anchel and his brothers, were active in various labor struggles against the owners of the Powazki slaughterhouse.[50] Moshe Kruk, a slaughterhouse owner, wrote in his diary about the Kolniczanski's and made references to their fights against the owners of the slaughterhouses. The tactics employed against Kruk must have had an effect because he filed a complaint against the Kolniczanski's. [51]

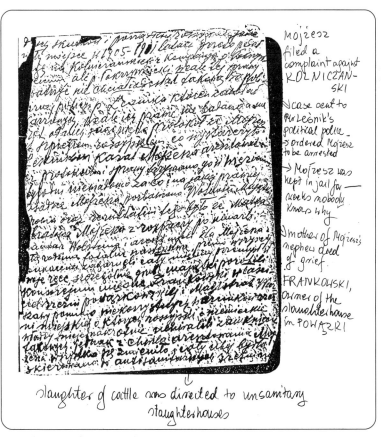

From the diary of Moshe Kruk

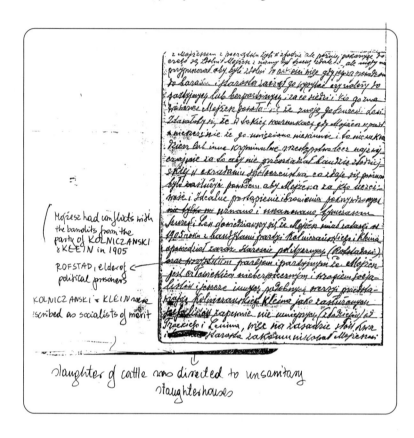

Kruk fought against the Kolniczanski's suppporters, whom he identified as "bandits." [52] His references to the Kolniczanski's are important not only as additional evidence of their involvement in labor socialist causes but in providing a date when the events took place in 1905.

There is one comment Kruk made in his diary, which contains an insight as to how the Kolniczanski's fought against the owners of the slaughterhouses. The comment refers to the kind of socialists the Kolniczanski's were, that is, "socialists of merit." [53] I believe this is an acknowledgement on Kruk's part that the Kolniczanski's were fighting for principles they believed in.

Anchel also was active in nationalist-revolutionary causes. There is a reference to his PPS (Polish Socialist Party) activities: "There were four brothers: Anchel, Itche,Yoshke and Motke. The oldest and the leader of them was Anchel. In his youth, he had belonged to the PPS...and was a PPS fighter. For a certain period of time, he belonged to the SS Povenzek group..."[54]

The actual meaning of SS refers to the Zionist-Socialist party, "formally organized at the Sixth Zionist Congress in February 1905."[55] They were advocates of a Jewish homeland and identified with socialist principles. The practical work of the SS in Powazki was its involvement in forming a labor union to represent the meat workers under the name 'united.'

In the years 1906-1907, the SS (which later became the main basis of the 'United,') organized a group of meat workers in the Warsaw suburb of Povenzek, where a large slaughterhouse existed.[56]

A police report clearly spells out the actions Anchel took to promote the union.

> . . .Arrested K., L. and Z. are one of the main figures in the union of butchers. They took personal part in the imposition and taking "fines" from the persons, which were under boycott by the union of butchers, threatening them by death and they also forced the meat-sellers to give work for workers, which were sent by the union, and they make, with guns in their hands, to leave the city, the persons which were unpleasant for the union.They did their measures with outstanding resolution. [57]

The K, L and Z refers to Shimon-Anchel Kolniczanski, Itsek Levenkorn, (nicknamed "Iche") and Srul Zilbersthtein (nicknamed "Zhultity").

That report can also be understood as an indication that Anchel was engaged in a power struggle against forces hostile to the union and that the

> struggles over political turf inside the factories were frequently resolved by the threat or use of physical violence, especially once the working class parties recruited more authentic factory workers, whose traditional method of persuasion was the closed fist. [58]

At the time of his involvement, ". . .the trade union movement embraced thirty-two thousand workers; of these, twenty thousand belonged to a political party." [59]

For the SS and later on, the United, as it came to be known, increased control over the union began during WWI with the building of the main slaughterhouse and the union's presence there.

> During the first world war, the SS made contact with the Povonzek meat workers and when the central slaughterhouse was built in Praga, and the meat workers union was created, this party already existed under the name "United." They had an influence upon the trade union and considered themselves as the political owners of the Union. [60]

In addition to Anchel's labor organizing efforts, he was very active in the movement for Polish independence through his association with the Polish Socialist Party.

Anchel had an elite status in the P.P.S. as a rifleman. "In the P.P.S. fighting squad, he was among the best marksmen." [61] These fighting squads were first formed in May 1905 and had a number of goals "to oppose the police and to instill greater discipline and self-confidence in the working class so as to strengthen its resistance to mobilization." [62]

Anchel's training as a rifleman took place outside Poland. "The Union sponsored the establishment of riflemen's unions in various Galician towns, taking advantage of an Austrian law which permitted the formation of para-military societies." [63]

As a marksman, Anchel was associated with that part of the P.P.S., which was engaged with armed struggle, known as the union of active struggle. [64]

Anchel was active in fighting against counterrevolutionary elements who were supporting the Tsarist authorities. "In 1905, during the revolutionary ambush on the 'muddy houses,' (houses of ill repute) and while fighting with the owners of these house keepers, Anchel was the most active participant among the revolutionaries." [65] The actions taken by Anchel and other revolutionaries was unplanned, ". . .an extraordinary spontaneous campaign against criminal elements suspected of collaboration. Brothels were ransacked, gang leaders were lynched." [66]

It is possible to pinpoint when Anchel's participation in these attacks took place: "Beginning in the Jewish quarter on May 24 and then spreading to Christian neighborhoods, the next day, crowds of workers attacked pimps, prostitutes and houses of ill repute throughout the city." [67]

```
7)   - Koln.            24 L
     - Anzelm           20
   ó Anzelm   1.VIII.1906
     - Anzel  wynagrodzenie   - 143,10.-
     - Anzel  rozjazdy        -  41,25.-
     - Anzelm utrzymanie      -  50,25.-
     - Anzelm               49,15.-
     - rachunek za wrzesień - Ignac 1
               Anzelm    - 225.-
     - Anzel  rozjazdy        -  15.-
     - Anzelm utrzymanie      -  35.-
     - Kol.  rpzchód          -  23,83.-


          - Koln.            24 L
          - Anzelm           20
          - Anzelm   1. VIII.  1906
          - Anzel   compensation    - 143.10. -
          - Anzel   travels (trips) -  41.25  -
          - Anzelm  upkeep          -  50.25. -
          - Anzelm             49.15 -
          - Account for September - Ignac 1
                    Anzelm   225.-
          - Anzel   travels (trips) -  15. -
          - Anzelm  upkeep          -  35.-
          - Kol.    expenditures    -  23.83. -
```

Document on Anchel's wages.

Anchel should be considered a professional revolutionary in the sense that he was paid for his activities.[68]

In 1908, Anchel and his comrades were arrested. At the end of October in the beer store in the Novo-Pikaya Street, five were arrested, self-willed, returned from exile terrorists: Shimon-Anchel K. (nickname 'Anchel'), Itsek Levenkorn (the nickname 'Iche') and Srul Zilbershtein (nickname "Zhultity").[69]

It is apparent that at the time of his arrest, Anchel was categorized as a political prisoner. In all likelihood, after his arrest, he was sent to either a local jail or prison for an extended period. After he was found guilty, he remained confined until his place of exile was determined.

Anchel was caught and ". . . for his revolutionary activities, he was sent to Siberia."[70] In the report on his exile, a significant fact appears: ". . .after consideration in the special conference, the circumstances from the dossier about arrested Anschel Moshkov Kolniczanski, was charged with belonging to the Jewish group of the party named "Proletariat." [71] That reference points to the fact that Anchel belonged to P.P.S. Proletariat, "founded in July 1900 by the Secessionists, a group of P.P.S. activists, who separated from the foreign section of the Lwow branch of the party in May 1900."[72]

The report not only identified the nature of Anchel's political activities, it also determined his punishment in relation to his political crimes. At the time, there were distinct classifications of political offenses:

> Political prisoners, whose crimes did not embrace theft or the destruction of life or property, but were involved in such activities as strikes, demonstrations, printing, distributing or possessing illegal literature, or being friendly to known opponents of the government, were usually exiled to Siberia for one year or longer. When they arrived at their place of exile, usually a village or a small town, they were allowed to rent a place to live and to find work. In addition, they received about a ruble a month for basic subsistence. However, they were required to report daily to the local police. [73]

With the imposition of martial law from 1905-9, as the principal means by which the Russian government put down rebellion in the Kingdom of Poland, Anchel's exile to Siberia was a direct result of the sweeping powers given to the Warsaw governor-general. Anchel's case was, in all likelihood, turned over to a field court ". . .established on an ad hoc basis and made up of a Chairman and four officers. The accused were to be tried within twenty-four hours of their arrest, with sentences passed no later than forty-eight hours after the court had convened. The proceedings were to be entirely secret, and the sentence, once submitted to and approved by the Commander of the military region (in the Kingdom's case, the Warsaw governor-general). . ." [74]

In 1908, the year of Anchel's trial, his acts were among many committed against the Russian government by the PPS. "By party affiliation, of those accused of political crimes against the state, 167 belonged to the PPS. . ." [75] Anchel was an obvious target of the field court, given his membership in the Union of Active Struggle. His ties to the PPS as a rifleman made him an enemy of the military government which was engaged in an effort to prevent weapons from "...falling into the hands of the fighting organizations of the political parties."[76] The police files refer to Anchel as a terrorist, an important concern for the governor-general of Warsaw.

Anchel's deportation to Siberia began in 1908 for two years, but a chain of events including Anchel's attempts to escape because of illness in the family extended his exile.[77]

```
                                   ... a letter from  the
   Departament of Police from the 15 of march,  1908. They wrote,
   that after  consideration  in  the  Special  Conference  the
   circumstanses from   the   dossier   about   arrested   Anshel
   Moshkov(i.e. son of Moschko -  A.V.)  Kolnichansky(so  in  the
   document - A.V.),  which  was  charged  with belonging to the
   jewish group of the party,   named "Proletariat",  the Miniuster
   of internal  affairs stated:  to deport Kolchanskyi(so in the
   document - A.V.) to the Arkhangelsk gubernia  for  two  years,
   since the 10th of march,  1908".  According to the desision of
   Arkhangel goventor,  he was  places for living to  the  village
   Ustkozha of the Onega ouezd,  where he was sent after arriving
   to Onega at the 6th of june, 1908.
        In the  report,   dated 15th of july,  1908,  Onega police
   cheif informed the goventor,  that at the 10th of july,  1908,
   Anshel K.  went into hidding to the unknown direction.  He put
   down his tokens:  " 22years old,  the height more then common,
   the eyes  hazel,   the  hairs,  brows  and  moustaches  dark-
   light-brown".
        At the 30th of december,  1908,  the Department of Police
   sent a letter to Arkhangelsk  goventor,  where  there  was  a
   desision of  a  minister  of internal affairs to exile K.  for
   THREE years,  since the 15th of Dec.,  1908, because he hidden
   from the pervious place of deport.
        At the 19th of february,  1909 he was  transported  under
   guard("po etapu")  from  Warsawa  and  was put into Arkhangels
   prison, as hidden from the place of previous deport, and then,
```

The following pages document Anchel's exile

by the desision of Arkhangels goventor, was sent to the Kem'
ouezd, where he was deported under the guards at the 22th of
march, 1909. Whilke being in exiling in the Kem ouezd, firstly
in the village of Kalgalaksha, then - in Hukhche, K. wrote
several appeal   to   the .goventor about his removing to
Arkhangels or Arkhangels ouezd, because his term of exiling
will end at the 15th of Dec., 1911 and, because of large
family, he has no money for long distance till the railway
station in winter way.

Answering to K. pleadings, the Arkhangels goventor
ordered at the 17th of jule to remove him to the town of
Kholmogory, and then he permitted him to live in SArkhangels,
where he arrived at the 5th of October, 1911, but from the
town of Kem and stayed in the hoyse of Andrukhin in the first
part, in the Kostromskoy prospekt(avenue).

The appeal of K. from the 11th of November, 1911, about
his pre-time freedoming because his wife illness was remained
without satisfaction.

From the message of Arkhangelsk city police departament
from the 17th of november, 1911, the Ministry of Internal
affairs "recognized as possible the pleading of the middle
class person of the village of Povonzky of the Warsawa
gubernia Ancheka Moshkova K. about his searching for·adoption
to military service or for his enrolling to the militiamen in
Akhangelsk military board instead of Warsawa military board
after ending of his exiling.

At the 29th of Nov., 1911, the cheif of Arkhangelsk
police informed to the goventor, that K. at the 19th of Nov.,
1911 moved away from Arkhangels to the uknown direction and
didn't returned till that time.

In the report from the 5th of february, 1912, Arkhangel police cheif inform the goventor, that K. voluntary returned from the running and stayed for living in the first part of the city, in the house of Ferber, N 72, by the St.-Petersburg prospect.

From the copy of the protokol, made at the 3th of febryary, 1912, by the duty police officer in the Arkhangelsk city police departament is followed, that in november, 1911, K. received from the motherland message, that his wife became very ill. He appealed to the staff of Arkhangelsk goventor for the permission to go home, but they refused him, because it's nesessary to senbt appeal to the ministry of internal affairs. Because it can take a very long time, K. desided to attend motherland without permission and after it re returned to the place of exiling, in Arkhangelsk.

Acccording to the order of goventor from the 9th of february, 1912 the rest of the time of exiling K. live in Arkhangelsk. In the report from the 2th of march, 1912, the chief of Arkhangelsk police departament let know to the Arkhangelsk goventor, that Anshel K. was freedom from the exiling because the end of his term and after it was removed to the Akrhangelsk local military board.

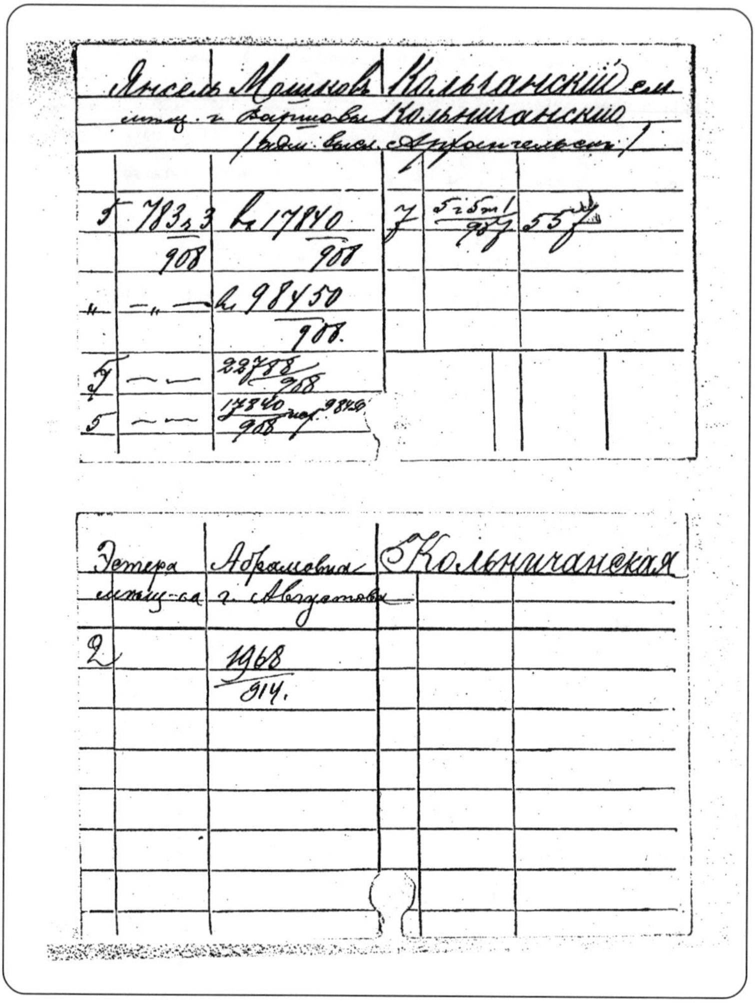
Янкель Мошков Кольчанский сн.
мещ. г. Варшавы Кольничанский
(вид. выс. Архангельск.)
5 783 23 17840/908 7 5 г. 6 т. 1/907 55
4 — 98450/908.
7 — 22788/908
5 — 17840/908 пер. 9849

Эстера Абрамовна Кольничанская
мещ-ка г. Августова
2 1968/914.

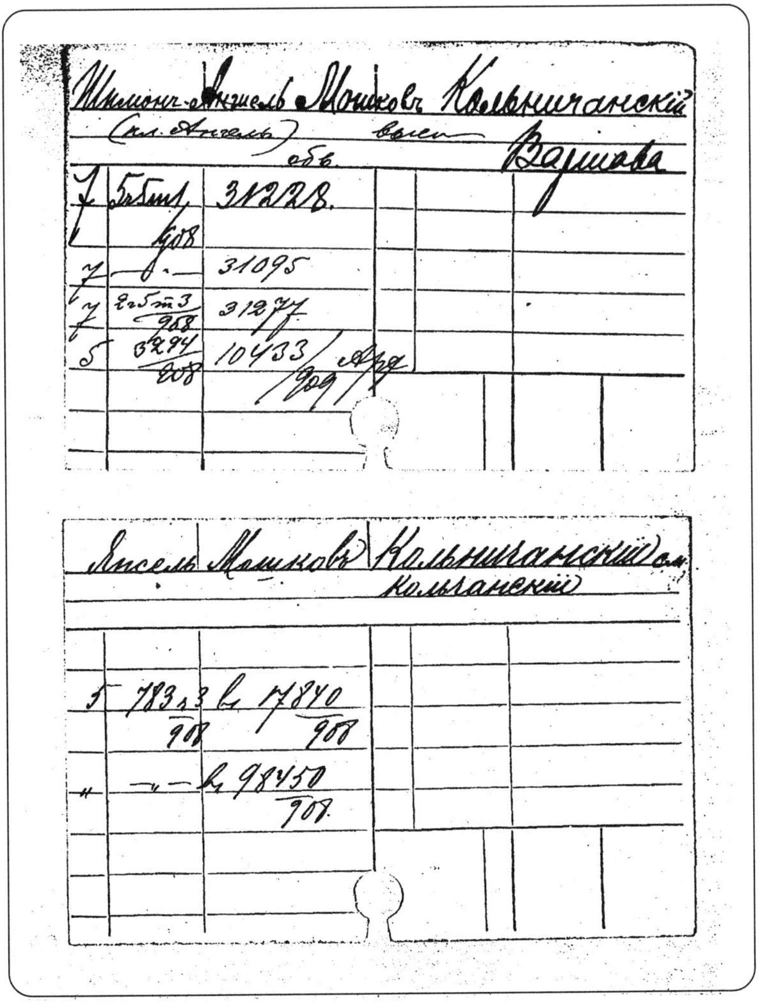
Шимонъ-Анзель Мошковъ Кальничанский

Варшава

31228.

908

31095

908

31277

908

10433

909

Ансель Мошковъ Кальничанский

Кальчанский

17840

908

98450

908.

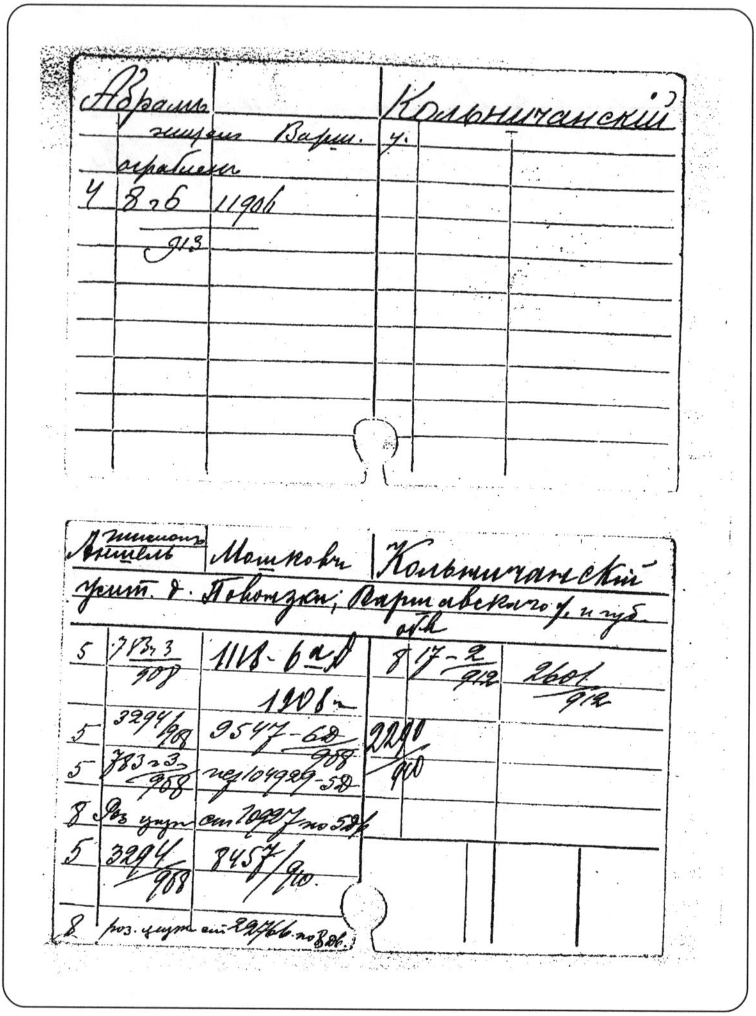

10927. Аншель Мошковъ КОЛЬНИЧАН-СКІИ.
а) ж. д. Поводзки гм. Млоцины Варшав. у. хл.
20 л. г) р. в. ср. тѣлосл. плт. в. т. рус. г. кар.
е) спр. Онежск. у. ж) пст. М. В. Д. 10 Мар. 08 г.
з) всл. Архангельс. г. 2 г. і) ар. об. ув. Архангельс.
Г-ра. к) V—783 и ѲК 08 г.

А. 22766. Аншель Мошковъ
КОЛЬНИЧАНСКІИ.
а) м. гм. Повонзки, Варш. г. и у., 23 л.,
іуд. б) от. Мошекъ, мт. Браня Мендель—гм.
Повонзки. в) бр. Шимонъ, Хаимъ, Рувель-
Ицикъ, Іосекъ, Мошка, сс. Шифха—при род.
г) р. ср., гл. кар., в. чер. е) скр. г. Арханг.
19 Нояб. 11 г., евр. парт. „Пролетаріатъ“.
ж) пст. М. В. Д. в) всл. нщз. Арханг. г. 3 г.
съ 15 Дек. 08 г. і) ар. об. прпр. расп. Арханг. Плцмст. и ув. Арханг. Г-ра. к) VШ—
22617.

The details of Anchel's romance and marriage to Fela, provides further proof of how he was motivated to follow his own thoughts in spite of strong opposition.

> He fell in love with the daughter of a slaughterer (shochet). The shochet was an honorable and extremely religious person and refused to hear about a marriage between his daughter and a common slaughterer and a former convict. Her parents were afraid that the daughter would meet secretly with her lover, and kept her home, not allowing her to walk into the street. But, this loving couple handled the situation according to all romantic rules. Anchel snatched his beloved through the window of the second floor. They eloped, married and lived happily ever after. [78]

All of Anchel's actions up to and during the Nazi occupation of Warsaw demonstrate his commitment to stay and fight in his native land. This was not the case with two other Kolniczanski's, Simon and Hyman. They, in effect, chose not to fight but to flee, to emigrate when confronted with anti-Jewish mesures.

In the case of Simon Kolniczanski, there exists an ample combination of documents and testimony which provide a clear picture of how he lived in Powazki and why he left for Denmark. What makes the Danish citizenship documents so accurate is that they were written in the words of the applicant. In his own words, he describes how, at age 14, "he became an apprentice shoemaker with his father, with whom he worked until 1899. . ."[79] Simon then went out on his own and "worked for 5 years in different places in Warsaw, and from 1904 he had his own workshop in Warszawa."[80] His motivation to leave Powazki was explained during my interview of Esther Spilok in Paris in January 1997. She spoke of a very typical reason why Jews left Poland: the pogroms. Simon states in his application that he arrived in Copenhagen on January 26, 1911.[81]Pogroms were not uncommon in the Warsaw gubernia [82] prior to 1911.

Esther Spilok's testimony demonstrates the essence of genealogical research, the stories, which breathe life into dates and events. For example, she explained in lively detail the following event, that turned out to be quite prophetic:

> One day, the children came upstairs and told our mother (Leah) to go downstairs because there was a fortune-teller who wanted to talk to them about their future. The children were curious and insisted. The palm reader told them that their mother would never eat a piece of salt with her husband in Poland. The reason was that he would go to another country, a country with a cold climate, and she would follow in the new country, where they would

have two more children. The fortune teller said she would go back to Poland as would her husband, but they would never visit Poland together. [83]

As it turned out, Simon emigrated to Copenhagen, arriving in January 1911, his wife and children arrived in August. Esther told me that her mother did not have enough money for a direct passage to Copenhagen, only as far as Berlin. In order to purchase the additional fare for Copenhagen, she had to sell her only pair of diamond earrings.

From the census records of 1916, it is learned that Simon Kolniczanski was a shoemaker, working at a shoe factory in Copenhagen.[84] According

Simon Kolniczanski's family photo, 1927
  Left Front: Justina, Esther, Leah, Simon
  Left Back: Israel Poula
  Others not identified

to Esther Spilok, he eventually started his own shoe repair business in the Jewish section of Copenhagen known as Prinsea's Gade, as of 1917. She remarked with lament that he was always "a poor man." His wife worked with him in his shop, which he had for 23 years.

Esther also spoke about the occupations of her sisters and brother.

Ida and Justina worked in a clothing factory, making clothes. Poula was employed as a maid, cleaning houses. Israel (Esther's brother) was a butcher.

In the case of Hyman Kolniczanski, documents and the testimony of his daughter Celia Russell, made it possible to construct some basic ideas as to why he left Poland and his life after he arrived in the United States.

According to Celia, Hyman had been studying to become a rabbi. In contrast to Jacob, Hyman and his family left Poland to escape serving in the Russian Army. The family did not go directly to the United States. Hyman was in contact with his brother Reuven. He emigrated first to Paris, where Reuven taught him the pocketbook business. His date of arrival in France was December 1912. A document from the Prefecture de Police proves he was working in Paris in 1913 as a pocketbook worker.

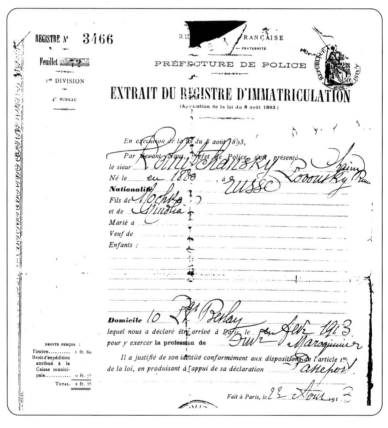

The family would eventually leave Paris for London, living and working there in the years 1914-16. In London, Hymie worked in a leather
factory. His wife, Lena, had learned how to do embroidery. This trade
would be of enormous help once they reached the United States. They
left London for New York in 1916. Hyman emigrated first on the SS New
York on July 22, 1916.[85] Lena departed for New York with the children on
November 20, 1916.[86]

The arrival of the Kolniczanski family in the United States was part
of a much larger wave of Jewish immigration. They were a part of the ". .
.more than 73% of Jewish immigrants to the United States between 1880-
1920, who came from the Pale of settlement. . ."[87] The fact that Hyman
and his family settled in New York as a family is consistent with another
trend, that Jewish immigration was "a movement of families."[88] New York
was the center of Jewish immigration during this period and the lower
east side for the years between 1890 and 1910 was the first place of residence. But the Kolniczanski's did not fit this trend. They would reside
first in the Bronx and then in the Washington Heights section of Man-
hattan. At first, Hymie worked in a pocketbook and leather factory. Per-
suaded by Lena, (who knew about embroidery), Hymie opened his first
store on Boston Road in the Bronx.

The Kolniczanski's were one step removed from what was the common commerce of immigrant Jews: peddling. They had their first store
from 1920-31, while living on Tinton Avenue. The second store was in
Washington Heights on 184th Street and Audobon Avenue. Both stores
sold fabric, buttons and other sewing notions. According to Celia, they
both felt the contrast between the "new land" and the old, a typical feeling for new immigrants. They were lonely for the large family they left in
Warsaw. Also, they missed the concerts, lectures, synogogues and holi-
day celebrations.

NOTES

[44] Bernard Goldstein, <u>Twenty Years in the Jewish Labor Bund</u>, p. 67. Chapters 17, 18, 25 and 27 of this book contain numerous references to the Kolniczanski family. Many important details, which were unavailable either through testimony or archival sources were obtained from this book. The translations of chapters in this book, from Yiddish to English, were done by Adele Miller.

[45] French National Archives.

[46]David Weinberg, <u>A Community on Trial: The Jews of Paris in the 1930s</u> (Chicago: University of Chicago Press, 1984) p. 3

[47]Ibid

[48]Goldstein, p. 65

[49]Robotnik, Organ Polskiej Partyi Socyalistyccz Nej, October 1, 1899, N 33

[50]I am thankful to Rita Krakower Margolis for providing sections of a relative's diary. In the diary, the owner of the Powazki slaughterhouse, Moshe Kruk, refers to the Kolniczanski's and their union activities, on pp. 49 and 58.

[51] Ibid, p. 49

[52] Ibid, p. 58

[53]Ibid

[54]Goldstein, p. 65

[55]Henry Tobias, <u>The Jewish Bund in Russia</u>, California: Stanford University Press, 1972, p. 322

[56]Goldstein, p. 60

[57]The report, the "7th Department of the Warsaw Department of Police," 1908, File 2, Part 5, Vol. 3, was obtained from the Archangel Archive. Anton Valdine assisted in researching the archives and translated documents from Russian into English.

[58]Robert Blobaum, <u>Revolucja, Russian Poland 1904-1907</u>, Ithaca: Cornell University Press, 1995, p. 100

[59]Ibid, p. 73

[60]Goldstein, p. 60

[61]Goldstein, p. 66

[62]Piotr Wandycz, <u>The Lands of Partitioned Poland, 1795-1918</u> University of Washington Press, 1974, p. 309

[63]Aleksandr Gieysztoz, Stephen Kienicwicz, <u>A History of Poland</u>, (Warsaw: Polish Scientific Publishers, 1979) p. 507

[64]Ibid, p. 508

[65]Goldstein, p. 66

[66]Norman Davies, A History of Poland, p. 372 (Columbia University Press, NY, 1982)

[67] Blobaum, p.94

[68]This reference was located in the State Archives of New Acts in Warsaw, microfilm NR 15 1256/12-20 of P.P.S. battle group accounts for the year 1906.

[69]"7th Department of the Warsaw Department of Police," 1908,

[70]Goldstein, p. 66

[71]"7th Department of the Warsaw Department of Police," 1908,

[72]Janusz Suserki "The Relation of the Polish Socialist Party: Proletariat to the Bund and the Jewish Question, 1900-1906" in Poles, Jews, Socialists: The Failure of an Ideal ed. Anthony Polonsky, Israel Bartal, Gershon Hundert, Magdalena Opalski and Jerzy Tomaszewski (London: The Littman Library of Jewish Civilization, 1996) p. 32

[73]Philip Desind, Jewish and Russian Revolutionaries Exiled to Siberia 1901-1914 (United Kingdom: Edwin Mellen Press, 1990) p. 84

[74]Blobaum, 279

[75]Blobaum, 280

[76] Blobaum, 282

[77]7th Department of the Warsaw Department of Police," 1908

[78]Goldstein, p. 67

[79]Application for Citizenship for Simon Kolniczanski was obtained from the Danish Archives. Translation from Danish to English was done by Arne Knudby.

[80]Ibid

[81]Ibid

[82]A small sample of pogroms in the Warsaw province illustrate this point. The American Jewish Yearbook for the years 1906-1907 on pp. 43, 45, 47 and 51 identifies with specific dates pogroms that occurred in the Warsaw province. In the years 1903-1906, pogroms in general were numerous, planned in advance and the victims knew when one was about to occur. See Klier and Lambroza, ed. Pogroms: Anti-Jewish Violence in Modern Russian History (England: Cambridge University Press, 1992). In the years, 1905-6, there were 15 pogroms in Poland, resulting in 452 deaths. Also the classic study by Leo Motzkin, Die Judenpogrome in Russland.

[83]Testimony of Esther Spilok, Paris, France, December 1996

[84]Danish archives

[85] Passenger list, Hyman Kolniczanski, U.S. Department of Immigration

[86]Passenger list

[87]Gerald Sorin <u>A Time for Building: The Third Migration, 1880-1920</u> (Baltimore: John Hopkins University Press, 1992) p. 12

[88]Ibid, p. 39

CHAPTER FOUR

The Slaughterhouse, WW I
and a Landsmanschaft

I N 1914, the members of the Kolniczanski family were well-estab-
lished in Warsaw, Paris and Copenhagen. In Warsaw, Anchel and
his brothers were well-off from their role as meat merchants in
the Praga slaughterhouse. In Paris, Reuven joined the French Army
at the start of World War I; in Copenhagen, Simon was among
those responsible for the formation of Jodisk Handvaerkerforening — a
landsmanschaft.

Detailed material exists on the Kolniczanski presence in the Praga
slaughterhouse. Praga, at the time, was considered a suburb of Warsaw.
Physically separated from the city by the Vistula River and connected by
a bridge, Praga presented a strong contrast to Warsaw. "The life there was
more provincial, more pleasant. The streets were broad, broken here and
there by large, empty spaces overgrown with grass, or even large sections
of field; there could be found here and there small, peasant courtyards
where chickens strolled around and pigs grazed."[89]

A Jewish business presence in Praga began in the middle of the 18th
century and by the 19th century, "...there were 5,000 Jews out of 6,700
inhabitants."[90]

Praga was known as a cross-road for Jewish commerce from surrounding towns. It developed as a marketplace "...for agricultural produce, cattle
and horses for sale and with money for buying goods for daily use — equip-
ment, clothing and products not produced by villages."[91] Praga was home

to crowded stalls, shops large and small, granaries and storehouses.

Praga also was well-known as a center of industry, in particular, the meat industry.

The Kolniczanski business presence in Praga begins with the completion of a new central slaughterhouse.

> When the slaughterhouses in the Warsaw suburbs were liquidated, and a central slaughterhouse was established in Praga, the Kolniczanskis entered the Praga slaughterhouse and became the people of authority.[92]

It is possible to pinpoint when it appeared. "The Russians have started to build the slaughterhouse, the Germans, however, completed it during their occupation."[93] In other words, "the slaughterhouse was developed and modernized in the period between World War I and War II."[94] The small slaughterhouses were dismantled: "all the previous slaughterhouses (in Povonzek, Okhote, Shilets and Volye) were liquidated at

The Slaughter Hall

The Wholesale Hall

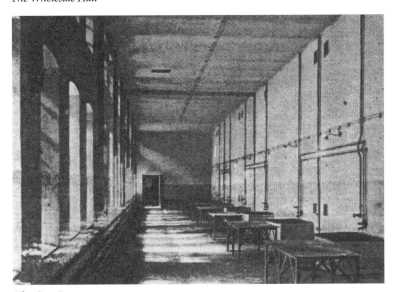

The Guts Room

The Refrigerator Hall

that time. . ."[95] It is estimated that "over a thousand people worked in a nearby slaughterhouse, among them 600-700 Jewish meat workers."[96] The Praga slaughterhouse processed meat for merchants, the city, the state, hospitals and the military.[97]

There is no doubt that the material gathered for the book Twenty Years with the Jewish Labor Bund on the Kolniczanski family and its involvement in the meat business was by someone who knew them personally. Consider the following quotes, one concerning the author's association with the Meat Trade Union: "Some of them I knew during the time I worked in Praga, some I knew from previous periods. For instance, the meat wholesaler Anchel Kolniczanski, who had a large influence in the slaughterhouse and in the Union."[98]

Additional evidence that the writer wrote a firsthand account of the Kolniczanski's appears in this quote: "through Anchel I was able to come closer to the Kolniczanski dynasty."[99] Anchel's influence was, in part, the result of his earlier efforts in Powazki to form a meat workers union. His control over the union in the Praga slaughterhouse began during the first world war, when ". . .the SS made contact with the Povonzek meat workers and when the central slaughterhouse was built in Praga, and the meat workers union was created, this party already existed under the name United."[100]

The union consisted of several sections, "slaughterhouse workers, workers handling kosher and non-kosher meats, sausage makers . . ."[101] The Kolniczanski's had control over the slaughterhouse workers, whose work was divided into the following sections, each with different tasks:

> . . .drivers who chased the ox and other animals from the railroad station to the stables. They were fed until they were taken to be slaughtered. Skin removers or the actual slaughterers were the most important and qualified workers. They stacked the dead animals on a pole and removed the skin. They cleaned the inside of the animal, but in half and quarters and completed this skilled work. They brought the cut skins to a special place where skin dealers came and purchased the skins. Record-keepers wrote down the amounts meat butchers bought and how much the butchers owed. Carriers brought the cut pieces or half of the animal to the carts. Drivers drove the carts and distributed the meat to the butchers in the town. There were workers who handled unusable parts of the animals and a section that handled calf.[102]

The Kolniczanski's class standing changed from meat workers to meat merchants during World War I. The reason for this change can be easily explained: "During the first World War, under the German Occupation, Anchel together with his brothers became an important smuggler of meat and in this way earned a considerable amount. When the war ended, Anchel was a man of great wealth."[103]

Meat smuggling during the German occupation only partially explains the privileged position the Kolniczanski family acquired in the Praga slaughterhouse. Other crucial factors were Anchel's past political ties and associations in the period of Polish independence.

> In independent Poland, he became a merchant dealing in oxen. He was greatly helped by his past revolutionary P.P.S. experiences, especially because he had been exiled to Siberia. Former fighters for Poland's independence, especially those who had served sentences in Siberia, such as the former convicts, were now a privileged group. Anchel had many friends among former comrades from the Polish Socialist Party, who now held very high government positions. For him, all doors of the national offices were open to him. This resulted in his becoming one of the decision makers at the Warsaw oxen and meat markets.[104]

Everyone associated with the slaughterhouse started the day early.

Outside the Slaughterhouse, 1936: (Archiwum Dokumentacji Mechanicznej)

> At 5 a.m., the street becomes alive, with wagons waiting to distribute meat throughout the city, and with meat merchants, butchers, drivers and slaughterhouse workers. All of them trying to reach the building of red brick near Namiestnikowska Street, the Praga slaughterhouse.[105]

The following description explains what was involved in the retail sale of meat.

> When you come to the building of the Slaughterhouse, you approach a huge hall filled with stalls where parts of oxen and calf carcasses are kept. Each of the stalls belonged to another meat merchant. Here, butchers come to buy meat for their butcher shops. In Warsaw were several hundred shops, kosher and non-kosher. In this hall, people dressed in white are running around, these are the veterinarians who inspect the animals before they are killed and who stamp the meat after the slaughter. [106]

The Kolniczanski's, like other meat retailers, had a place in the slaughterhouse, where their animals were slaughtered. For Jewish butchers, oxen and cattle had to be slaughtered in accordance with strict Talmudic rules, which required that the animals had to be killed in a certain manner and they had to die quickly. Sick animals were excluded from slaughter. The number of animals slaughtered was determined by whether a merchant had a small or large business. "Big merchants slaughtered several hundred animals per week, small merchants several dozen per week."[107] On average, about "50 oxen were being slaughtered at the same time in different corners."[108]

The description of activities inside the slaughterhouse conveys the intensity of the work environment where the Kolniczanski's had their retail meat business.

> The shouting in the hall is very loud. The butchers are talking in loud voices. After they purchased the meat, one can hear screaming: "Yosel take my meat!" "Yankel take it down!" "Chatzkel take my quarter first!" And to make their voices stronger, they curse as they usually do. Mixed with the screaming of the merchants, is heard roaring of the oxen, pigs, calves, cows kept closed in the nearby stalls. In the nearby hall, howling is heard from the oxen that resist being slaughtered and refuse to move. So they drag the ox and pull him from all sides. The driver makes wild noises, but is deafened by the horrible roaring of the oxen being slaughtered. About 50 oxen are being slaughtered at the same time in different corners. Different voices are mixed in a frightening, hellish sound. One has a feeling of fear, which one experiences when coming into the slaughterhouse for the first time. More fear is felt when you come into the slaughterhouse hall. The roaring of the oxen as they are bound become more frightful. Blood runs into canals, which finally flow into a central canal, (the blood is then collected and sold for different purposes).[109]

The slaughterhouse workers went about their task of killing and processing the animals following a set routine.

> The slaughterhouse workers are standing in deep leather or rubber boots in water, wearing long leather aprons with sharp knives in their hands. They are completely covered with blood, sweat is running from their faces. With long glittering knives, they flay the oxen which are then hung up on bars. With huge axes, they split the animal first in half, then in quarters. The sight of the just slaughtered animal creates a terrible fear. He is tossing, kicking

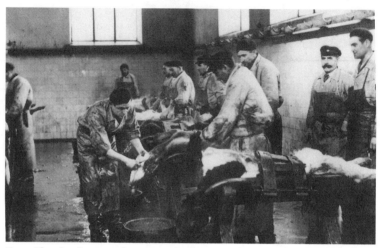

Praga Slaughterhouse workers, 1936: (Archiwum Dokumentacji Mechanicznej)

with his feet, and it seems as though he is jumping in your face. The entire work is done in a horrible uproar as workers are unable to talk to each other and have to shout in loud voices in this wild tumult. [110]

Their grisly daily task of slaughtering, cutting up and disposing of animal parts made for a highly charged, intense work atmosphere.

> The slaughterhouse workers, Poles and Jews, were often slightly drunk. They found it difficult to work on a sober stomach. Always smeared with blood, they were easily roused to a fight, but they never lost their heads. The sign of an impending brawl was the clanging of the bloody knives on the stone floor as they pulled them out of their boots and tossed them away. No one wanted to kill a comrade in the heat of a fight. [111]

The slaughterhouse workers were a very colorful group, intense in how they lived and worked. Their energetic and powerful presence can best be illustrated by a comparison with other workers:

> There comes to mind a comparison between the meat handlers and the bakers. They worked nights almost at the same time. Bakers worked all night and returned home in the morning. The meat workers started their work in early morning hours and finished at midday. But what was the comparison between them? The baker was a depressed, weak, pale sickly man, as against the meat worker,

Workers remove skin from an ox, Slaughterhouse, 1936: (Archiwum Dokumentacji Mechanicznej)

who was bloody, healthy with big shoulders with a red face. They lived in Warsaw in the same neighborhood on Smotche, Niska, Wolinska and Krochmalna. They were often seen together but what a contrast in spirit, moods and posture. [112]

The everyday operations of the slaughterhouse were in many ways the product of the political influence of the Kolniczanski family. Anchel's political connections and past activism with the meat union translated into his having direct control over many of the activities in the slaughter-house. "Anchel's authority was great not only among the meat merchants, but also with the entire Meat Workers Union. Everyone listened to him and he even involved himself in the internal quarrels among members of the union." [113] Anchel's involvement and control over the Meat Union benefited his meat business: "Although he was an employer and a mer-chant, the Union extended special privileges to him. He was allowed to pay lower wages for the butchering of his oxen and the union had no choice but to go along with these privileges, because Anchel's power was so great." [114]

Of the four Kolniczanski brothers involved in the meat business, Anchel was the undisputed one in charge. Anchel's influence had defi-nite benefits for his brothers Icie, Yoskie and Motke who were involved in the meat business as union officials.

> His three brothers benefited from their brother's authority and
> they too had great influence among the meat handlers. They also
> had an important voice in Meat Workers Union's affairs and in
> the slaughter-house. All three were members of the union's man-
> agement; and all three were clearly representatives and each had a
> large portion of the 'pool.' They did not have to work hard. Yoskie
> represented the section of the hide carriers; Motke handled the
> kosher meat dealers, and Icie the meat carriers. [115]

The hide and meat carriers whom Yoskie and Icie supervised
performed essential services to the functioning of the Praga slaughterhouse:

> They cleaned the inside of the animal, cut it in half and quarters
> and completed this skilled work. They brought the cut skins to a
> special place where skin dealers came and purchased the skins...
> Carriers brought the cut pieces or half of the animal to the cars.
> [116]

The Kolniczanski's extended their influence in the slaughterhouse
to their brother-in-law who married their sister Shifra. "The brothers
helped their brother-in-law, Leizer Schnichter, their sister's husband. He
received a monopoly for handling a great number of wagons for distrib-
uting meat from the slaughterhouse. This was his dowry."[117]

In other words, Leizer Schnichter was in charge of both the drivers
and the distribution of meat to the various butchers in Warsaw.

In essence, the profits the Kolniczanski's derived were the direct result of how the 'pool' was divided. The division of the pool is a striking
example of the influence the Kolniczanski's had.

> In each section, the work was done on a cooperative basis. Every-
> thing they earned was put into a "pool" and at the end of the
> week every member of a section came and received a part of money
> due him, not according to qualifications but to an arrangement
> they made between themselves. A representative from the meat
> union was assigned to every section. This representative did not
> have any authority over the section, but he received a part of the
> money from the pool, and also received money for expenses which
> supposedly were covering his leadership. The representative from
> the management was not from the same section. Often, he was a
> member of another section. This person received salaries from
> two pools. From one where he was a representative, and the sec-

ond where he was a member. Often, this was a person who worked in his section only several hours per week, as he was busy being a representative in another section. So, he received two salaries and often quite larges ones from both pools. The tenure of the management of the union and representatives to the sections were held by three old meat families, three dynasties who had the authority over the entire union, over the trade at the entire Warsaw slaughterhouse.[118]

The "three old meat families" refers in part to the Kolniczanski brothers, who had a large say in the running of the slaughterhouse. The two other meat dynasties were the Chayatchkes and the Bertchikes families. [119]

The power the Kolniczanski's, the Chayatchkes and the Bertchikes families had in the slaughterhouse extended not only to control over the meat union, but also to the buying and selling of meat. The author's first-hand knowledge of the three families can best be understood by this quote:

> A special role was the fact that I did not take advantage of my friendship with the meat handlers for material gains. I quickly won the confidence of the entire meat trade. They started inviting me to their family celebrations. They asked my advice in family matters. They told me about their family troubles, what was on their mind, as one would to a close relation. [120]

Of the three meat dynasties, the Kolniczanski's were the most powerful: "the largest and strongest meat dynasty was the family Kolniczanski, who came from the Warsaw suburb of Povonzek." [121]

How long the Kolniczanski's remained in control of the meat union is not known. What is known is that as of the summer of 1924, the family lost its leadership positions to the Chayatchkes. "It was shortly after the election of a new board of the Meat Worker Union in which the Chayatchkes defeated the Kolniczanskis that Shmuel Gabai was selected a president of the union." [122]

Other prominent meat retailers, such as the Bertchikes, attended a celebration sponsored by the Chayatchke family as well as "the entire board of the meat workers, except the Kolniczanski's." [123] It is easy to understand why the Kolniczanski's would not attend. Nonetheless, they were upset at Goldstein's presence at the party and the use of union property. "The Kolniczanski's carried a grudge against me because I went to the celebration. But they would not say this openly. They reproached me for allowing the union orchestra to be used at a private celebration."[124]

Anchel's upper-class standing had obvious effects on social ties and on his family. "His home became a meeting place for the town intelligentsia. His two daughters and son attended high school (gimnazjum), spoke Polish and acted like rich children."[125]

The fact that Anchel's children attended a "gimnazjum" was a clear indication of the family's social standing. At the time, a high school education was neither mandatory nor free. The gimnazjum was clearly an elite and privileged institution. Nonetheless, it was a common aspiration to attend. Given the admission restrictions placed on Jews seeking admittance to public high schools, Anchel's children in all likelihood went to a private high school. For parents and children, a gimnazjum education provided a modern outlook and was regarded as a passage to higher status.

The family read <u>Nasz Przeglad</u>, founded in 1923, a newspaper that appealed to secular Jews. By and large, the paper defended Jewish interests and had a strong pro-Zionist bent. Most often, Anchel's daughters, in particular, Guta, submitted to the magazine section answers to the crossword puzzles. [126]

While his brothers in Poland had achieved economic success, Reuven (now Robert) was making his own mark in a new country, the most important symbol of which was fighting for France in World War I. My mother on those relevant occasions would comment at length about Robert's war record. In particular, she spoke about his sense of pride in having fought and survived the war. It provided him with an identification with France as his home. This has been described as a typical feeling for many Eastern European immigrants. "The war provided the Jews with an opportunity to write in blood their love for France and to engage in political activity on behalf of the fatherland." [127]

At the time that Germany declared war on France (August 3, 1914), "there was a spontaneous movement among Jewish immigrants to join and fight against the Germans." [128]

Robert fought in World War I from 1914-1918. Archival documents, photographs and the testimony of my mother and aunt establish his length of service. He served in the 2eme regiment Mixte de Zouaves et Tirailleurs, 48eme division. His name is listed in the Gold book of soldiers of Verdun in France, number 19257. One of the many medals he received was the medal of Verdun inscribed with the well-known expression "Ils ne

Reuven Kolnitchanski, seated right, holding a 1907 St. Etienne machine gun.

Source: Combatant de la Guerre

Robert Kolnitchanski in the Zoaves uniform

passeront pas!"
This photograph shows
Robert with his uniform
early in the war. [129]
His Zouave uniform,
which he wore early on, had
many distinctive features:

The headgear is the
chechia, sometimes
worn with a cover of
blue cloth, in a shade
similar to that of the
line infantry's Kepi
cover, issued from Sep-
tember 1914. The rest
of the uniform con-
sisted of a short, collar-
less jacket, with a
coloured loop (tombo)
in the braid to distin-
guish the four Zouave
regiments (garance,
white, jonquil yellow
and light blue, respec-
tively). This was worn
over a sleeveless vest
(sedria) in the same
colours, and around the
waist was a broad cum-
merbund. Both white
cotton or garance cloth
baggy sarouel trousers
were worn in France... [130]

As regiments de marche, the Zouaves et Tirailleurs consisted of "regiments de marche, composed of a mixture of active, reserve and newly-
raised battalions. This resulted in nine regiments de marche de Zouaves,
two regiments de marche d'Afrique (one a Zouaves/Foreign Legion formation, the second all Zouaves) four regiments de marche mixtes de
Zouaves et Tirailleurs and 20 regiments de marche de Tirailleurs." [131]
    The Zouave regiments were known for their savage attacks and for
some time, were considered an elite force. Another photograph has Robert in the first uniform issued in 1914. This uniform was redesigned, so,

Robert Kolnitchanski in the 1914
uniform

Robert Kolnitchanski in the 1915
uniform

based on a "decision of April 21, 1915"[132] Robert wore a new uniform.

Robert received medals and a citation. One was the Croix de Guerre, which was given for heroism. "The Croix de Guerre was instituted on April 8, 1915. It was open to soldiers and sailors of all ranks. . .and was mentioned in a dispatch from an officer commanding an army, corps, division, brigade or regiment."[133] Robert's medal is referred to as a divisional dispatch due to the silver star on the ribbon. He also received the Croix du Combattant, a medal symbolizing his service in the French Army and in the war.

It was the citation he received on November 13, 1918 that best illustrates the courage he demonstrated as a chasseur. According to documents concerning his citation, Robert was assigned to a Foreign Legion branch of the Zouave, a Polish regiment. He was assigned for an obvious reason, his fluency in the Polish language. There are two other reasons

This citation refers to Robert's role as a runner.

why he was assigned and served in that branch as of 1915: "Heavy losses in action and the repatriation of men of Allied nations with their own armies forced a reorganisation, and in 1915, these regiments were all amalgamated into the formidable regiment de marche de la Legion Etrangere. . ."[134]

Robert's task was especially life-threatening. When communication all too often broke down, messages were relayed by the chasseurs, who had to run between the trenches as relay runners. Subjected to consistent enemy fire, the casualty rate for the relay runners was very high.

An archival source of five books, Le Journal de Marche du Regiment in Vincennes contains a day by day account of the 2eme Regiment Mixte de Zouaves et Tirailleurs. Le Journal de Marche provides an account of the specific battles in which Robert participated. For example, his regiment fought four times in Verdun, in February, April and May 1916 and August 1917. Robert was wounded on May 17, 1916 in front of Douaument. The 2eme Regiment fought in many well-known and bloody

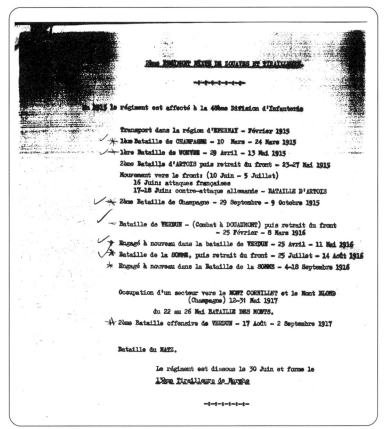

2eme regimente mixte de Zouaves

battles of the war.

The day by day, hour by hour accounts in the Journal des Marches provide a terrifying image of what my grandfather and his regiment had to confront. There were the references to the Champagne campaign. The Regiment arrived to participate in the battle on March 13: "At 10 p.m., heavy bombardment with 5 killed and 5 wounded." At 3 a.m., on March 16, the 2eme Regiment was given the order to join another regiment and attack the enemy trenches. They were able to advance 400 meters, before they had to retreat to the point of origin. The following day, starting at 6 a.m. they faced a brutal German counterattack, made all the more terrifying by the widespread use of hand grenades.

On March 20th, they were subjected to intense bombardment from

3 p.m. until 10 p.m. This was an all-too-common tactic used by all sides to break down morale. The bombardments in this instance were so intense that they reshaped the French trenches. This is a significant fact, if one considers that "the most common cause of battle casualties when in the trenches was enemy artillery fire." [135]

The journal entries for September 29th and 30th contain an account of the daily activities in the trenches during the Champagne campaign. On September 29, helmets and bayonets were distributed. The cleaners were at work in the trenches. The next day, there was intense bombardment. German machine guns were on the high ground and greeted all movement in the trenches with machine gunfire.

At the battle of Woevre, the 2eme regiment dealt with similarly intense and brutal confrontations with the enemy. On April 29, the troops were prepared for a 5 a.m. attack. The Germans were aware of the impending attack and subjected the troops to an intense bombardment. The attack made an advance of 100 meters and was halted by barbed wire. They were forced to retreat. Such a small advance proves how close the French and German front lines were. As the 2eme regiment retreated, it was subjected to machine gunfire, suffering many casualties. A second assault on the German positions had the same results. The 2eme regiment's participation in the best known battle of the War, Verdun. The Journal des Marches contains for the most part references to troop movements, not day to day battles of my grandfather's regiment.

In one period, the 2eme regiment fought in Verdun from February 25 to March 8, 1916. Both the Journal des Marches and secondary sources offer some details regarding the regiment's role in the battle. From the journal, it is known that the regiment was, as of February 24, placed on alert and units were assigned the task of reconnaissance. The regiment was mobilized at 1 p.m. and at 2:30, departed for the front. On that day, the regiment sustained heavy losses and the next day, the French 24th regiment ". . .burst into a vacuum left by the Zouaves that had melted away the previous day." [136]

The Journal documented the large number of Zouaves killed and wounded at Verdun. Prior to the 2eme regiment's redeployment, they were subjected to a heavy bombardment by German planes on March 8th. In the Regiment's second return to Verdun, they once again suffered heavy losses.

My grandfather's name is among the list of wounded soldiers in front of Fort Douaumont on May 17, 1916.

It's not at all surprising that he was wounded, the Germans were well-aware of an attack to retake Fort Douaument: "Within 48 hours, the

Germans knew every detail. All their offensive projects were immediately suspended and work began urgently on patching up Douaumont's defenses." [137] When the French troops prepared to leave the trenches, German guns were ready ". . .and as the first French soldier went over the top a murderously accurate counter barrage swept the whole line." [138]

For the wounded, the first problem was to receive medical attention. Troops were not allowed to provide medical care during an advance. All too often, the wounded had to wait for the stretcher-bearers.

> On leaving the aid post, the wounded soldier was taken by bearer to an advance dressing station where again little surgery was attempted. Unless there was a need to control a haemorrhage, remove a smashed limb, or give initial treatment for gas poisoning, the patient was again sent on his way as quickly as possible, either by motor ambulance or ambulance train. His next destination was a casualty clearing station and it was in these that most of the surgery was done. [139]

A French soldier who was wounded would fall into one of three categories: "those who would die anyway, and were not worth operating on; those who would probably survive, but would be of no further use to the war effort, and those who could eventually be returned to duty." [140] I have no information as to what kind of wound my grandfather sustained, just the end result, which was that he survived and returned to active duty. He was fortunate to receive the Croix de Guerre and live to talk about it. Unfortunately, there were many soldiers who received the medal and did not. ". . .it had become a recognised custom to reward a man about to die with the Croix de Guerre." [141]

Verdun's infamous reputation is well-deserved. One estimate put the casualties on both sides at more than 700,000. [142] The battle also has the distinction of being the war's longest, ten months. It claimed the highest number of casualties. Because of the intensity of the bombing, nothing grows there to this day. It was almost impossible to recover for burial all the bodies strewn throughout the battlefield. The day in, day out, shelling was so intense that the dead on the battlefield were ". . .quartered and requartered, to one eye-witness it seemed as if it were filled with dismembered limbs that no one could or would bury." [143]

I wonder how my grandfather coped with this calculated insanity, which drove many soldiers to simply break down. At the very least, he must have responded like so many other soldiers: "a private in one of the four crack French corps who was at Douaumont in the Verdun battle told his parents that by the ninth day [of the barrage], almost every soldier was crying." [144] It would be a sad irony that Robert often remarked to my mother, "I survived Verdun," in reference to the German occupation in World War II, as if to dismiss its importance.

The Journal des Marches contains a detailed description of the 2eme regiment's role in La Somme. There is the reference to July 28th, a bright clear day, characterized by an intense bombardment of large caliber shells. The following day, there is violent cannon fire. A striking description of the atmosphere and violence of this battle appears in the account of July 30 from 5:45 a.m. The attack unfolds as a mass of men in motion faced with a violent barrage of bullets whistling at them as they attempt to surge forward. My aunt remembers my grandfather telling her, "when you hear the bullets, it is not dangerous for you. When you do not hear it, the bullet is for you." Movements were in a fog so thick you could not see the enemy fire. As the French troops made some forward progress, the grisly task of clearing out the bodies of the dead from the battlefield had to be performed. From this sample of my grandfather's troop's experiences in World War I, it is easy to understand why he thought the German occupation of France during the second world war paled in comparison to what he lived through in the first world war.

If ever there was a lasting memory, which embodied how my grandfather remembered World War I, it is his telling of the story of the "Tranchee des Barionnettes." He spoke of the terrible fate of the 137th infantry regiment, who died standing at their posts in the trenches, buried alive, bayonets protruding from their rifles. This cannot be verified, but what is beyond dispute is how this story illustrated for my grandfather the horror of that war and what it meant to him to have survived.

Another illustration of what my grandfather went through during the first world war are the collective citations proposed for the 2eme regimen, one in July 1915 and the other in September 1916.

Headquarters, Commander in Chief of the Tenth Army
July 11, 1915
Collective Citations

From 2eme Regiment Mixte Zouaves et Tirailleurs Army degrees Number 88

The General Commander of the 10th Army cites "a l'ordre de l'armee," the 24th Army Corps and also the 48th and 58th division, which under the general Commander in Chief, for outstanding performance during renewed attacks, over a few consecutive weeks and under intense and continuous shelling, day and night, by the enemy artillery, they proved themselves with tenacity and self-sacrifice above all praise.

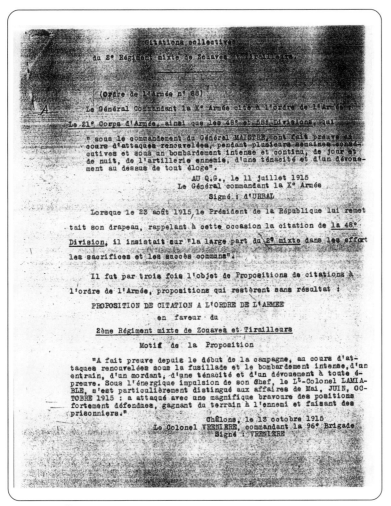

Citations Collective

For the 48th Division:
September 27, 1916
Motive of the proposition

Since the beginning of the campaign, proved themselves, notably in Verdun, during several attacks, full of determination and tenacity, self-

PROPOSITION DE CITATION A L'ORDRE DE L'ARMEE

en faveur du

2ème Régiment mixte de Zouaves et Tirailleurs

Motif de la Proposition

"A fait preuve depuis le début de la campagne, au cours de nombreuses attaques, d'un entrain, d'un mordant, d'une ténacité et d'un dévouement à toute épreuve. Sous le commandement de son chef en Colonel LAMIABLE, vient de donner toute sa mesure dans un secteur violemment bombardé, soit en attaquant, soit dans l'exécution de toutes les missions qui lui ont été conférées, faisant preuve de la plus grande abnégation et provoquant l'admiration de tous les Chefs qui l'ont eu sous leurs ordres.

Verdun, le 17 mai 1916
Le Général BULLEUX, commandant la 96e Brigade
Signé : BULLEUX

PROPOSITION DE CITATION A L'ORDRE DE L'ARMEE

en faveur du

2ème Régiment mixte de Zouaves et Tirailleurs

Motif de la Proposition

"A fait preuve depuis le début de la campagne, notamment sous Verdun, au cours de nombreuses attaques, d'un entrain, d'un mordant, d'une ténacité et d'un dévouement à toute épreuve.
Sous l'énergique impulsion de son Chef, le Lieutenant-Colonel LAMIABLE, s'est particulièrement distingué aux affaires d'août et septembre 1916 sur le front de la Somme.
A attaqué avec une magnifique bravoure des positions fortement défendues, enlevant de haute lutte 5 tranchées allemandes et gagnant du terrain à l'ennemi sur une profondeur de plus de 1.500 mètres. A pris 3 mitrailleuses; 1 minenwerfer et fait plus de 200 prisonniers.

Somme, le 27 septembre 1916
Le Général LAROQUE, Commandant l'Infanterie de la 48e Division

Signé : LAROQUE .

Citations Collective

sacrifice above all else.

Under the energetic initiatives of the Chief, Colonel Lamible, they distinguished themselves concerning the matter of the Somme front from August to September 1916. Attacked with magnificent bravery, strongly held positions, taking out 5 German trenches, through intense combat, penetrating 1,500 meters of enemy territory, taking three machine guns, one mine sweeper and taking more than 200 prisoners.

Somme, September 27, 1916
Le General Laroque
Commander, 48th infantry division

The souvenirs Robert brought back from the war leave little doubt as to the intensity and up close, personal nature of the fighting. Among the items that my mother said were in their apartment in Paris, were, in addition to his helmet and rifle, a German luger and a binocular with the name of a German officer inscribed on it. The last items were two artillery shells from Verdun. Robert had had the word "Verdun" engraved on the shells.

In contrast to Robert, Simon Kolniczanski's pursuits in Copenhagen were peaceful. Esther Spilok in a February 3, 1997 letter brought to my attention her father's role as a founder of what she described as a "Jewish society," or Landsmanschaft, known as Jodisk Handvaerkerforening. Simon was one of five founding members of the society, established in January 1914. He remained a member of the governing board, appearing in a 1919 photograph. As of 1932, he was listed as a member.

The society continues to exist to this day. Jodisk Handvaerkerforening's history appears in a work on eastern European Jews in Copenhagen.[145] "As of January 1914, 20 members were registered. The fee was 10 kr for membership and then 20 ore per week."[146] The society fulfilled many of the typical functions of a landsmanschaft, providing a range of social activities and function, which ultimately serve two purposes, to maintain ties to the old country and to allow for adjustments to be made to live in the new country. In part, the motivation to form Jodisk Handvaerferforening was to provide an alternative to two other societies for immigrant Jews known at the time as the Club of the Taylors and the Central Bureau. The tension between established and immigrant Jews was a common occurrence not only in Denmark. The classic example in the United States illustrates the tension between the established German Jews and incoming eastern European Jews in the 1880's. The society Jacob helped to form was, in effect, an alternative to the established organizations, for the poorer, eastern European Jews. Regarding Jodisk Haandvaerferforening, the eastern European Jews of Copenhagen, looked at the Central Bureau as "a Danish-Jewish organizations, and therefore they wanted, as the new Jews from the East, to prove that they were able to take care of themselves."[147]

Membership list, 1932, Jodisk Handvaerkerforening

The Society founded by Simon Kolniczanski (Simon is 2nd from left, back row)

Notes

[89]Goldstein, p. 9

[90]Marian Fuks <u>Zydzi w Warszawie</u>, Poznan: Daszewice 1992, p. 211

[91]Ibid, P. 212

[92]Goldstein, p. 66

[93]Goldstein, p. 9

[94]Goldstein, p. 10

[95]Ibid

[96]Goldstein, p. 100

[97]Goldstein, p. 60

[98]Goldstein, p. 99

[99]Goldstein, p. 60

[100]Goldstein, p. 63

[101]Goldstein, p. 63

[102]Goldstein, p. 64

[103]Goldstein, p. 67

[104]Ibid

[105]Goldstein, p. 96

[106]Ibid

[107]Goldstein, p. 63

[108]Goldstein, p.97

[109]Ibid

[110]Goldstein, p.97-98

[111]Bernard Goldstein, <u>Five Years in the Warsaw Ghetto</u> (New York: Doubleday, 1961) p. 15

[112] Goldstein, <u>Twenty Years in the Jewish Labor Bund</u>, p. 99

[113]Goldstein, <u>Bund</u> p. 66

[114]Goldstein, <u>Bund</u> p. 67-68

[115]<u>Bund</u> p. 68

[116] <u>Bund</u> p. 98

[117]<u>Bund</u> p. 69

[118]<u>Bund</u> p. 64

[119]<u>Bund</u> p. 99

[120]Bund, p. 99

[121]Bund p. 66

[122] Bund, p. 104

[123] Ibid

[124] Ibid

[125] Bund, p. 67

[126]The names of Anchel's children appear in Nasz Przeglad Ilustrowany: Dodatek Specjaxny do NR 288, Naszejo Przegla du NR 10 14, NR 22

[127]Paula Hyman, From Dreyfus to Vichy: The Remaking of French Jewry 1906-1939 (New York: Columbia Press, 1979) p. 50

[128] Images de Memoire Juive, Paris: Editions Liana Levi, 1994 p. 96

[129] Ian Sumner and Gerry Embleton, The French Army 1914-1918 (London: Reed Books, 1995) p. 43

[130] Ibid, p. 35

[131] Ibid, p. 8

[132] Ibid, p. 14

[133]John Luffin, A Western Front Companion 1914-1918 (United Kingdom: Alan Sutton Publishing, 1995) p. 172

[134]Sumner and Embleton, p. 10

[135]John Ellis, Eye Deep in Hell, Baltimore: Johns Hopkins University Press, p. 61

[136]Alistair Horne, The Price of Glory: Verdun 1916 London: Penguin Books, 1993, p. 109

[137]Horne, p. 236

[138]Horne, p. 238

[139]Ellis, p. 110

[140]Horne, p. 66

[141]Horne, p. 185

[142]Horne, p. 327

[143]Horne, p. 175

[144]Ellis, p. 65

[145]Bent Bludnikow Eastern European Jews in Copenhagen 1904-1920 (Copenhagen: Transaction Press, 1986) p. 50

[146]Ibid, p. 122

[147]Ibid

CHAPTER FIVE

Success and Foreboding Signs

F OR THE KOLNICZANSKI FAMILY in different parts of the
world, the decades of the twenties and thirties were a period of
transition, in both a positive and negative sense. There were
similarities and differences in the economic standing of sib-
lings who emigrated and those who remained in Poland. For
instance, Simon Kolniczanski, as Esther Spilok stated, was "a poor man,"
who struggled to make ends meet, as a worker in a shoe factory in
Copenhagen and then managing his own shoe store. On the other hand,
Hyman Kolniczanski was improving his material condition as his second
store was turning consistent profits. For the Kolniczanski's of Warsaw, a
clear indicator of their economic well-being are the photographs that
were taken of the family in the year 1925. The photographs, known as
"carte de visite" and "cabinet portrait" demonstrate that the Kolniczanski's
were, like others who could afford them, "the wealthy subjects of so many
of the early portraits (who) had sought out and paid handsomely for the

(These photographs show the brothers in 1925, left front:
Robert, Anchel, Leizer; left back: Joskie, Icie, Motke; a
separate photo shows the sister, Shifra

services of the artistic studio photographers."[148]

One way to understand the economic standing of the Kolniczanski
family of Paris is through a discussion of the Powonski Society.[149] Simon
was not the only Kolniczanski who was involved in forming a
landsmanschaft. In Paris, Robert formed the Powonski Society. There were
and still are clear class divisions among the various landsmanschaftn. My
Aunt Natalie (nee Kolnitchanski), married David Luxemberg, who was a
member of the Radom Society, a well-known, large landsmanschaft repre-
senting Jews of high economic standing. This became clear to me when I
visited the Bagneux cemetery, outside Paris. The monuments for members
of the Radom Society are elaborate and well-maintained.

It is from the testimony of my aunt Mina and my mother that I first
became aware that Robert was the founder of the Powonski Society. Supporting archival evidence appears in a document obtained from Bagneux
Cemetary, which also makes it possible to appproximate the date when
he founded the society. That document shows that he purchased burial
plots on June 10, 1923,[150] a task usually reserved for the president of the
society. I suspect that my grandfather formed the society after returning
from the war, between 1919 and 1922. In his application for French citi-

This document indicates that Robert purchased burial plots for the Powazki Society.

zenship in 1913, the summary of his activities in France makes no mention of the Powazki Society. A year later, he joined the French Army. This tends to support my claim that the society was formed after the war. By 1923, the society had raised sufficient funds for the purchase of burial plots.

The other evidence is from a photograph from the year 1925 that my mother gave me of herself and her sister, when they were about six months old. Each of them is wearing a gold chain. As children of the society, they were given this gold chain with a heart, which displayed a star of David on the front. On the back was written "Societe Powonski." They often described the Powonski Society in sharp contrast to the Radom

Dora Kolnitchanski and the twins.

Mina and Helene wearing Powonski Society medals

Society as the "poor people's society."

My Aunt Mina has spoken of Robert's key role in the society not only as the founder but also as a provider of assistance to new immigrants from Powazki. In fact, Robert's society was so well-known in Powonski that travellers to France were advised, "when you go to Paris, go see Robert Kolnitchanski." She explained that they would go to their apartment and he would help them get the necessary papers and information for finding work, a place to live and other essential services.

Aunt Mina generously provided me with important documents that my grandmother had kept on the Powonski Society. One document is positive proof that the Powonski Society had merged with the Warsaw Society after 1945. Supporting evidence was found in the Report of General activity of societies affiliated with the federation of Jewish societies of France as of 1945. The Powonski is not listed, but the Warsaw Society is.[151] (Records acquired for the years 1931 and 1937 show that the society was at that time, independent and self-sufficient. [152]

Landsmanschaftn membership books are important historical documents in that they contain details on everything from the society's formation, conditions of membership, governance, as well as the social services the society provided. Chapter I, article 2 of the membership book for this society details the services it provided: 1) to allocate grants in case of sickness, injury or an accident; 2)to grant a subsidy for maternity; 3) to allocate grants to assist in the event of the death of a family member; 4) to help with the expenses of a funeral; and 5) to accord exceptional help in case of extreme emergency. Contained in Chapter 3 are detailed references to the composition of the society and conditions of

Liste des Associations et Groupements affiliés

A LA FEDERATION DES SOCIETES JUIVES DE FRANCE

47 Sociétés de Secours Mutuels

Agoudah
L'Aide Fraternelle
L'Amicale Israélite
Les Amis Solidaires
L'Avenir Fraternel
L'Avenir Mutuel
Bessarabia
Bikor Cholim de Montmartre
Les Bons Amis
Amicale de Brest-Litowak
Les Amis des Brocnnt de Belleville
Les Amis Solidaires de Brzeziny
Carreau du Temple
Chevra Kadischa
Czentochow
Le Devoir Fraternel
Enfants de Chrzanow
Enfants de la Prévoyance
Halvoyès Hamés
Hévré Thélim Vékadichlué
L'Humanité des Ouvriers du XI*
Gargan-Livry et Pavillons (La Fra-
ternelle)
Gobelins (Union Fraternelle des)
L'Internationale Progressiste

Les Israélites de Paris
Konsk (Les Amis de)
La Loi de Moïse
Lublin (Originaires de)
Morin (de Clichy)
Mon Repos
Odessa (Amicale d')
Les Ouvriers Tailleurs Modernes
Piotrokow (Les Amis de)
Powonski (Les Originaires de)
Praga (Les Originaires de)
Rowno (Les Originaires de)
Roumanie (Les Originaires de)
Russe (Amicale)
Salvé
Tomaszow Mazowiecki (Les A. du)
Transylvanie (La)
L'Union des Travailleurs (Agou-
dath Ahim l'oale Zedec)
Vigilante Israélite
Varsovie (Les Amis de)
Véracité
Volontaires Juifs
A. C. au service de la France
Zechor Abraham

UNION DES SOCIETES OSE   92 Avenue des Champs-Elysées

OZER DALIM   Palais de la Mutualité 24, rue St. Victor

POUR NOS ENFANTS   35 rue des Francs Bourgeois

LES ORIGINAIRES DE POWONSKI 5 rue Oberkampf

LE PRET SANS INTERET I place Sacco-Vanzetti,Clichy

Assoc. des ORIGINAIRES DE ROUMANIE 47 rue de la Victoire

SALVE   5, avenue de la République

LES AMIS DE TOMASZOW-MAZOWIECKI 159 rue de Belleville   (M. Leiblang)

TRADITION ISRAELITE   7 rue de Trétaigne

UNION DES PETITS COMMERCANTS   5 avenue de la République
    ET PETITS FABRICANTS JUIFS

UNION POPULAIRE JUIVE 10 bis, rue Elzévir

UNION DES TRAVAILLEURS 113 rue Damrémont   18°

TRANSYLVANIE 83 rue du Temple   3°

LES AMIS DE VARSOVIE 10 rue Dupetit-Thouars

VERITE ET GRACE   5, avenue de la République

Prefecture de Police records. These documents provide evidence of Powazki Society activity in the 1930s.

SOCIÉTÉ MUTUALISTE
Les Amis de Varsovie-Ochota-Powonski
Autorisée sous le N° 75-4504
Siège social : 14, rue de Paradis - PARIS (X°)

N° **185**

M - me. _Kolnitchauski._

Adresse _140 Rue_ _efem Cmontant_
Paris 20°

Profession ....

Le Président :   Le Secrétaire Général :

£ _Goldsly_

STATUTS

TITRE PREMIER

CHAPITRE PREMIER
FORMATION ET BUT DE LA SOCIETE

ARTICLE PREMIER. — Une Société Mutualiste est établie à Paris, 14, rue de Paradis, sous le titre : « Les Amis de Varsovie-Ochota-Powonski ».

ART. 2. — Elle a pour but :
1) D'allouer des secours en cas de maladies, blessures ou accidents ;
2) D'accorder une prime à la Maternité ;
3) D'accorder des secours en cas de décès ;
4) De pourvoir aux frais de funérailles ;
5) D'accorder des secours exceptionnels en cas de besoins urgents.

ART. 3. — Sont bénéficiaires :
Les membres participants et leur famille.

CHAPITRE II

COMPOSITION DE LA SOCIETE
CONDITIONS D'ADMISSION

ART. 4. — La Société se compose de membres honoraires et participants.

— 3 —

ART. 5. — Les membres honoraires sont ceux qui, par leurs souscriptions ou par des services équivalents, contribuent à la prospérité de la Société sans participation à ses avantages. Ils ne sont soumis à aucune condition d'âge ou de nationalité.

ART. 6. — Les membres participants sont ceux qui, en échange du paiement régulier de leurs cotisations, acquièrent ou font acquérir vacation aux avantages assurés par la Société, sans autre distinction que celle qui résulte des cotisations fournies, des risques apportés ou de la situation de famille.

ART. 7. — Peuvent adhérer à la Société les personnes qui remplissent les conditions suivantes :
1) Etre présenté par deux membres de la Société ;
2) Etre domicilié à Paris, dans la banlieue ou dans une province.

ART. 8. — Les membres participants et honoraires sont admis par le Conseil *à la majorité* des voix.

CHAPITRE III

ART. 9. — La Société est administrée par un Conseil composé de 8 membres élus au bulletin secret par l'Assemblée Générale.
Ces membres, qui sont obligatoirement choisis parmi les membres participants ou honoraires de la Société, doivent, pour les trois quarts au moins, être Français, majeurs, jouissant de leurs droits civils et civiques ; en aucun cas, le Conseil ne pourra comprendre plus d'un quart d'étrangers majeurs et n'ayant encouru aucune condamnation sur le territoire français.
Le Conseil doit comprendre au moins deux tiers de membres participants.

ART. 10. — Le bureau du Conseil d'Administration comprend un Président, deux Vice-Présidents, un Secrétaire, un Trésorier.

ART. 11. — Les membres du Conseil sont élus pour un an et sont renouvelés tous les ans.
Nul n'est élu au premier tour du scrutin s'il n'a reçu la majorité des suffrages. Au deuxième tour, l'élection a lieu à la majorité relative. Dans le cas où les candidats obtiendraient un nombre égal de voix, l'élection serait acquise au plus âgé.

ART. 12. — Le Président et les Membres du Bureau sont élus chaque année par l'Assemblée Générale.

ART. 13. — Le Président assure la régularité du fonctionnement de la Société conformément aux statuts. Il préside les réunions du Conseil et les Assemblées Générales, dont il assure l'ordre et la police. Il signe tous les actes de délibération. Il représente la Société en justice et dans tous les actes de la vie civile ; il fournit à l'autorité compétente, dans les trois premiers mois de chaque année, les renseignements statistiques et financiers prévus par l'article 25 de l'Ordonnance du 19 octobre 1945.
Les Vice-Présidents secondent le Président et le remplacent en cas d'empêchement.

ART. 14. — Le Secrétaire est chargé des convocations, de la rédaction des procès-verbaux, de la correspondance, de la conservation des archives, ainsi que de la tenue du registre matricule.

ART. 15. — Le Trésorier fait les recettes et les paiements ; il tient les livres de comptabilité.
Il est responsable des fonds et des titres de la Société. Il paie sur mandats visés par le Président ; il touche, avec l'autorisation du Conseil, toutes les sommes dues à

Les Amis de Varsovie-Ochota-Powonski booklet

admission. Articles 5 and 6 contain references to the goals of members in relation to benefits provided by the society. Admission requirements are found in Article 7, such as residence in Paris or nearby suburbs and an introduction by current members. The governance of the society is described in Chapter III; 8 members are elected by a secret ballot voted on by the general assembly. These members must have no police records.

There are two sections in the Bagneux cemetery, outside Paris, where members of the Powonski society are buried.

The twins often speak of how proud my grandmother was of her participation in the society's social events. In particular, there was the annual inaugural ball, a place for old friends to meet and for singles to socialize. This photograph shows my grandmother at an annual ball in

Powonski Society gravestones at Bagneux Cemetary

Dora Kolnitchanski with her son, Albert at a Powonski Society ball, 1950s

the 1950's. The location where the ball was held would change from year to year but it was always held in a big hotel. She was part of the reception committee that greeted people at the door and was in charge of collecting the entrance fees. She wore a pin that said "comite." My grandmother was well-suited for the task, Aunt Mina said, because she loved people.

She would say "Moi, j'aime les jeunes, l'aime le Monde."
My mother and Mina also speak with heartfelt emotion about their
father. He would outwardly project to others his great appreciation of
humor, always with a funny story. In no uncertain terms, he was someone who believed in set rules and a code of ethics. He had an optimism in
terms of how he judged people, always looking for the good side and not
searching for the negative. The portrait I have of him is of someone highly
cultivated and well-read. Robert read and spoke French, Polish and Russian in addition to Yiddish.

Robert's first wife, Hinda, had died during a miscarriage while he
was at the front. The civil records identify the date of her death as February 4, 1917. At the time of her death, Robert's two children, Natalie and
David, were placed in an orphanage for one year. Hinda had been buried
in Pantin Parisien, a Jewish cemetary in Paris. Documents acquired from
the Bagneux Cemetary show that he purchased a burial plot in Bagneux
for members of the Powonski Society. They also show that shortly after
making that purchase, Robert had her body exhumed so that it could be
buried there. He had made sure that she would be buried with others
from Powazki and where he would one day be buried, as far as I am concerned, an indication of his noble character.

My mother and Mina recall vividly how proud my grandfather was
of his two daughters, the twins as he called them; they said his face would
beam as he walked with them down the street. My mother conveyed to
me how he had a soft spot for his twins. When they did something wrong,
he would quickly forgive them. She recalls a story to illustrate this. One
evening, it was his intention to take
them to the opera. (His favorite operas
were Tosca and Pigicci). He was waiting for them at home and expressing
his displeasure to them because they
were late in coming home. When my
grandfather served the dinner, they
told him the soup was delicious and
asked him what was in it. He quickly
forgot his anger.

My grandparents met at a store
owned by Dora's father (Grouchka) at
23 rue Julien la Croix in 20 e. It was a
shoe repair store. The family lived in
the back of the store. They were married   in   January   1920.   My

*Wedding photograph of Dora and
Robert Kolnitchanski*

grandmother's first husband had died from a heart attack. She had one child at the time, Adolph, or Max, as he liked to be called. As an infant, Adolph had had the misfortune to suffer a fall (he was dropped by a babysitter) that injured one of his legs. The operation on his leg did not correct the injury and left him with a limp. Nonetheless, in other ways, Adolph had many advantages. He was self-taught in all things mechanical. My mother characterized him physically as good-looking and said that the girls "ran after him." In spite of his handicap, he was a very good dancer. In the 1930's, he opened his own repair shop in Paris and struggled to make a living at it.

The sharp economic differences between the Kolniczanski's of Warsaw and Paris became apparent to me as I learned how my grandparents made their living. My grandfather was a pocketbook maker with his own shop. In his shop he made luxury handbags, described by my mother as evening bags embroidered with silver and pearls. His main export market for the pocketbooks was the United States, but when the stock market crashed, he lost his business. In an effort to help make ends meet, my grandmother went into business. There was no doubt, my mother told me, of how gifted a businesswoman she was. She worked at the Carreaux du Temple, a famous retail market in Paris, where clothing, handbags and shoes were sold. It was known as a place for bargains and good mer-

Dora Kolnitchanski with pocketbooks, Carreux du Temple

chandise. Most of the merchants were Jewish.

In order to sell pocketbooks at the Carreaux du Temple, my grand-mother had to be licensed and registered by the Chamber of Commerce. Registration provided merchants with numbers that allowed them to sell their merchandise. There was a set time and procedure involved in the selling of pocketbooks. Typically, all activity began at 7:30 a.m. when the sellers arrived and places were assigned. Registration numbers of all the sellers were thrown into a basket, and stalls were assigned as each num-ber was pulled out. Then sellers began displaying their merchandise on tables. The Carreux opened for business at 9 a.m., by 1 p.m. all activity had ceased.

My grandmother's skill as a businesswoman can best be explained by this example: My mother said that a customer might have come to the Carreaux to buy a blue bag, but maybe she had none that day. It didn't matter. The customer would leave, having purchased instead a red bag from Dora and she would be very happy with her purchase. My grandmother's dream was to have her own store, but she never realized it. What was truly amazing was that she could not read or write. When people ordered merchandise, she remembered everything and tallied it all in her head.

In addition to selling pocketbooks at the Carreaux de Temple, my grandparents would frequently travel throughout France to sell pocket-books in open markets. They would "shlepp" their suitcases full of mer-chandise as they traveled from town to town. Very often, they would take a late evening train. Since they had no money for a hotel, they would sleep in the train station until morning.

The economic hardships were also felt at home. At times, my mother and Mina would arrive home after school to find that the lights in the apartment could not be turned on. My mother remembers she would simply say, "Oh, they cut the electricity again." Gas was worse, she re-members, because then they couldn't cook. In spite of these hardships, my grandparents would always manage to bring something back from their travels for the children. What is touching in all this testimony is the overall contentment and happiness my mother and Mina felt because they never felt a lack of affection and love from their parents and feeling content with anything they had. Everything was shared.

Robert's commitment to his life in Paris and to his family despite the economic hardships can best be illustrated by the fact that this brothers in Warsaw often urged him to return and they offered him a place in the family's meat business, but when he did return it was just to visit. In turn, his brothers visited him in Paris. Anchel's wife was in Paris in the 1930s and she visited with Dora and Robert.

Their work selling pocketbooks in the 1920s and 1930s was a typical occupation for Jewish immigrants in Paris. "...the most striking charac-

teristic of the professional distribution within the eastern European immigrant community was its heavy concentration of artisans."[153] These artisans had their own shops or worked at home. They counted for "almost 50 percent of all native Jews in Paris in the 1930s. . ."[154]

From 1925 until they fled Paris in the early 1940s, the family lived at 140 rue Menilmontant, staircase number 13, 2nd floor. Like many Parisian streets, it has a colorful history.[155]

Jews engaged in the trades in Paris generally lived in certain arrondissements. Belleville was one part of an area in the 20e, where Jewish artisans settled. They migrated, starting in the 1920s "peu a

Dora, Fela Kolniczanski (center) and Robert

140 Rue Menilmontant

Dora Kolnitchanski, left and Robert   *Israel and Lola Kolniczanski, Warsaw*
Kolnitchanski, right, selling pocketbooks *1934*

peu on grimpa plus haut, jusqu'a la hauteur de Menilmontant."[156] It is no
coincidence that the Kolniczanski family lived and worked in the 20 e.
The 20 e along with the 11 e and the 18 e had the highest concentration
of immigrants. What was also distinctive about the 20 e was the large
number of Polish-Jewish workers.

The middle years of the 1930s brought a sense of foreboding to the
Kolniczanski's. Two events stand out: the visit of Israel Kolniczanski,
Simon's son, to Warsaw and the emigration of Motke Kolniczanski to the
United States; both shed light on the anti-Semitism of that period.

Israel Kolniczanski traveled to Warsaw in 1934 from Denmark to
learn how to become a kosher butcher and he stayed with Anchel's family. In my correspondence with Danish relatives,[156] I learned of an incident in the Praga slaughterhouse that occurred when Israel was in the
company of Anchel. Someone had called out "Jew!" with derogatory references. Anchel sprang into action, grabbing knives and chasing the of-
fender over the rooftop, who eventually eluded Anchel. Israel commented
that "this happened very often." This was in the mid-1930s when Nazi
sympathizers and fascist organizations in Warsaw had a strong following
and were very visible. These groups included the anti-Semitic Endeks
and the fascist Falanga. At the time, the Polish government not only did

little to curb the activities of these organizations, it followed an anti-Semitic direction in part "to counteract the propaganda that it was a government of Jew-lovers." [157] There were boycotts of Jewish stores and violence against Jews. There were other actions taken against Warsaw's Jews:

> . . .attempts were made to drive the Jews from public parks and gardens. On the event of national holidays, pickets paraded in front of Jewish stores to prevent Poles from entering. At the beginning of the school year, Polish students were stopped at the doors of Jewish bookstores. In the university, the Polytechnic, and other higher schools, the Jewish students were not allowed to sit with Poles. Jewish pedestrians were attacked on the open streets. [158]

The rising tide of anti-Semitism would have a direct impact on the Kolniczanski's retail meat business at the Praga slaughterhouse. As of 1939, anti-Semitic legislation in the form of a bill designed to cancel the current system of slaughtering animals was fought by the Jews. The bill would prohibit the practice of slaughtering animals according to requirements of Jewish Kashruth (dietary laws). The overall intent was to remove the economic role Jews had in the meat industry, where the Jews had some influence.

These events and their significance did not go unnoticed by Motke Kolniczanski. The testimony given to me by my father and Aunt Bella concur as to why Motke and his family left Warsaw. Overall, it was his interpretation of internal events in Warsaw and events in Germany that led him to decide to leave. My grandfather had spoken to his brothers in telling them that "the Nazis will begin to persecute the Jews." His brothers listened but remained unmotivated to leave Poland.

It was no easy decision. Motke was one of the four Kolniczanski brothers who had an important economic role in the Praga slaughterhouse. His family lived in an upscale part of Warsaw at 36 Chlodna Street. He had fought with this brothers to establish their presence in the meat business and the union. My father remembers as a small boy, finding a gun in the apartment, hidden behind a furniture piece. My father explained that his father kept it "to deal with all the fighting in the meat industry." In terms of his family's material well-being, Motke had a lot to lose by emigrating from Warsaw, but he had made up his mind. They left Warsaw in 1933.

Their year of departure was well-timed. In 1933, Poland began to model Germany through the introduction of anti-Semitic measures. Germany was well-aware of this and encouraged it. "After the Nazis came

Motke Kolniczanski with my father, Morris, as a boy. Warsaw, 1930

to power in Germany, the German embassy and consulates in Poland followed all anti-Jewish manifestations throughout Poland with special interest and sent home detailed reports about them. German propaganda succeeded in making capital of Polish anti-Semitism and endeavored to portray the anti-German line in Poland as a "Jewish policy." [159]

Their first destination was Palestine. "Their emigration to Palestine in the 1930's was part of a trend, with more than one-third of Jewish immigrants from Poland at the time, choosing Palestine." [160] The family lived for one and one-half years in Tel Aviv at 32 Rehold Street. Not long after arriving there, Motke purchased a two-family house nearby at Rehold and Ali Jaf streets. There was a tenant and the space downstairs was rented for commercial purposes. But Palestine was not to be the family's final home. They ended up leaving Palestine for reasons similar to those that led to their emigration from Poland. This time, it was the increasing tension and conflicts among Arabs and the British. My grandfather said, "The Jews and Arabs will continue to fight."

Their final destination was New York. He left on the SS Olympic[161] by himself to find work and an apartment. Then he sent for the rest of the family.

The 1930's was not the best of times for the Olympic, one of those "floating palaces" built before the first world war. Times had changed;

the massive flow of immigrant traffic to the United States during the first two decades of the 20th century declined. Prior to the start of WWI, steamships like the Olympic transported more than one million people to America. [162] It was the fares of third-class passengers in the steerage quarters that had made the White Star company prosper. When my grandfather booked his passage in the Olympic in 1934, his third-class ticket did not mean as it had meant in previous decades, an accomodation in "bare steel bunks and almost sinister dormitories." [163] Instead, third class meant "cabins with attendants, stewards and an overall sense of comfort, cleanliness and ample ventilation." [164] The outward appearance of the Olympic at this time indicated a liner in decline. In its final years, the

The Olympic. Courtesy of the Steamship Historical Society of America Collection, Langsdale Library, Univ. of Baltimore

Olympic appeared "scarred in rust." One year after my grandfather arrived, the Olympic went to the scrapyard.

Upon arriving in New York, Motke Kolniczanski's name was shortened to Max Kolin. Hymie was the first to do this and Max was the second. At first, prior to the arrival of the rest of his family, he stayed at the apartment of the Yudowitz family on Union Avenue in the Bronx. Mrs. Yudowitz was his wife's mother. This was not entirely a matter of choice for him. There was the issue of U.S. immigration policy, which in the 1920s was designed to exclude large numbers of Jews from emigration to the U.S. It is ironic that my grandfather emigrated from Poland to Palestine only to once again confront anti-Semitism in the United States im-

migration laws. I suspect he must have thought that no matter where a
Jew went, he could not escape anti-Semitism.

Another issue that also was a part of restrictive immigration policies
was a directive issued by President Herbert Hoover on September 8, 1930,
calling for strict enforcement of "Likely to become a Public Charge" (LPC)
provision of the law. [165]

The effectiveness of Hoover's directive to the State Department had
the chilling effect of significantly diminishing Jewish immigration. For
example, in 1932, there was a dramatic decline from "the previous year's
242,000 to 35,000." [166] The immigration laws had broad popular support,
reflecting the reemergence of nativism. For instance, the populist anti-
Semitism of Catholic priest radio talk show host, Charles Coughlin and
the rabid anti-Semitism of Henry Ford, acquired respectability through
the exposure newspapers and members of Congress gave to their views.

> . . .the New York Daily News gave extensive space to speeches and
> pamphlets by Coughlin. . .anti-Semitism now had its spokesmen in
> Congress. Senator Robert Reynolds, Democrat of North Carolina,
> published a weekly newsletter, "American Vindicator," which bor-
> rowed extensively from Coughlin's "Social Justice. "Congressman
> Louis T. McFadden, Republican from Pennsylvania, quoted
> from...Henry Ford's 'International Jew' on the floor of the House." [167]

My grandfather had to prove that he and his family would not become public charges and that there were relatives who could assist his
family. This explains why he resided with Mrs. Yudowitz and why the
signature of his brother, Hyman, was on his immigration paperwork.

His family could not have arrived at a worse economic time, right in
the middle of the depression. They settled in the Tremont section, a part
of the East Bronx, where many of the depression's victims lived. ". . .the
residents endured protracted unemployment and extreme financial hardships, experiencing the collapse of American industry. . ." [168] Poverty and
misery was the lot of many East Bronx residents; many factory workers
also lived there. At the time, the East Bronx also was home to ". . .almost
half of the Jewish population of the Bronx." [169] The borough's Jewish population reached "585,000 in 1930, making up 48 percent of the Jewish population in New York City. "[170] The family lived at 1347 Prospect Avenue,
well-known as a working class neighborhood and having a large number
of eastern Jewish immigrants.

It is obvious that both of my grandfathers possessed an adventurous
spirit, in that they left behind a large family and comfortable surround-
ings to face the unknown in a new country. A strong memory I have of

Prospect Avenue, Bronx New York, 1938: Front L to R: Tillie and Max Kolin, Back L to R: Morris, Bella, Lily, Jack

my grandfather, Max, was of someone who projected joyful optimism and confidence. These traits served him well as he confronted the challenges of finding work and learning English. He could speak and read Yiddish and Polish. To learn English, he went to school three nights a week.

Finding work was a bigger challenge. At the Praga slaughterhouse, he played a management role in the labor union. He did not know how to work with his hands. His intention was to continue working in the meat business and he went about it with a considerable amount of chutz-pah, by simply walking into a butcher shop in the Bronx and telling the owner that he wanted to learn the trade. For his "lessons," he paid the butcher five dollars a week. In the early 1940's, he found steady work as a journeyman butcher, working for set periods of time at local butcher shops. Work assignments resulted from his membership in Local 342-50, the Kosher Butcher's Union, which was part of the UFCW, the United Food and Commercial Union. [171]To get work, he went to a hiring hall. The union provided me with a copy of his work history. The work was steady, but to make ends meet, other family members had to find work, too. My father made the difficult decision to leave school to find work. He never finished high school.

By the mid-1940's, the family's standard of living had improved, dem-

Work history for Motke Kolnitchanski in the U.S.

onstrated by their move to 30 Buchanan place in the West Bronx, just a few blocks off of the very prestigious section of the Grand Concourse, home to the Jewish middle class, including doctors, lawyers, schoolteachers and factory owners. The Kolin family had achieved a certain level of economic security.

The year 1938 was the last year of peace in Europe. In that year, the oldest Kolniczanski brother, Simon, died from cancer. He had had bronchitis and his doctor had told him to give up smoking, but he had been unable to do so. Simon was the last of the Kolniczanski's to perish during that period not from the actions of Nazi perpetrators, but from natural causes.

NOTES

[148]Lucjan Dobroszycki and Barbara Kirshenblatt-Gimblett Image Before My Eyes: A Photographic History of Jewish Life in Poland Before the Holocaust (New York: Shocken Books, 1977) pp. 9-10

[149]Given the number of landsmanshaftn that appeared in Paris, it is understandable that research on them, such as Jonathon Boyarin's book Polish Jews in Paris (Indiana: Bloomington Press, 1991) could overlook the Powonski Society. Also Boyarin informed me in correspondence that he was unaware that the Powonski Society had merged with the larger Warsaw Society, which was the basis of his research.

[150]Mairie de Paris, Direction des Parcs, Jardins et Espaces Verts, Service des Cimetieres, Cimetiere de Bagneux, Ref. 625/98

[151]Report number, 949D, Prefecture de Police file

[152]L'Almanach Juif 1931, Paris, La Nouvelle Generation, 1931, p. 189, and from Prefecture de Police, from a file on Federation de Societes Juives de France, January 7, 1938.

[153]Paula Hyman, From Dreyfus to Vichy: The Remaking of French Jewry 1906-1939 (New York: Columbia, 1979) p. 73

[154]David Weinberg, A Community on Trial: The Jews of Paris in the 1930s (Chicago: University of Chicago Press, 1984) p. 11

[155]The history of rue Menilmontant is described in Jacques Hillairet's Dictionaire Histories des Rues des Paris (Paris: Edition de Minuit, 1998) pp. 124-125

[156]Esther Spilok and Ketty Henning, Jacob's granddaughter, provided details of Israel's visit to Warsaw. The letters cited in the text are from Ketty Henning from fall 1996 and spring 1997.

[157]Five Years in the Warsaw Ghetto p. 19

[158]Ibid.

[159]Emanuel Melzer "Anitsemitism in the Last Years of the Second Polish Republic" in The Jews of Poland Between Two World Wars edited by Gutman, Mendelsohn et al. (Boston: University Press of New England, 1989) p. 136

[160]Joseph Marcus, Social and Political History: Jews in Poland, 1919-1939, New York: Mouton Publishers, 1983, p. 388

[161]The SS Olympic was the sister ship of the SS Titanic. Material on the SS Olympic appears in Eugene Smith's Passenger Ships of the World, Past and Present (Massachusetts: George Dean Co., 1952) pp. 193-194

[162]William Miller, Liner (Wellingbrough, England 1986, p. 12

[163]Ibid.

[164]Ibid.

[165] Howard Sachar, A History of Jews in America (New York: Vintage Press, 1992) p. 475

[166] Ibid, p. 456-457

[167] Beth Wenger, New York Jews and the Great Depression (New Haven: Yale University Press, 1996) p. 91

[168] Ibid

[169] Ibid, 92

[170] Bernard Postal, "A Short History of the Jews in the Bronx" Bronx County Historical Society Journal Vol. II, No. 1 January 1965

[171] Joseph Belsky, I, The Union: The Personalized Trade Union Story of the Hebrew Butcher's Union (New York: Raddock Brothers, 1952) is an interesting account of Local 342-50.

CHAPTER SIX

The Holocaust
Poland

S O MUCH CAN BE SAID and will be said about the fate of the
Kolniczanski family during the Holocaust. In essence, the discussion demonstrates the relation of place and fate. As their
family name was the product of place, so was their fate during
the Holocaust. For the Kolniczanski's of Warsaw, at different
times in different ways, both parents and children were murdered by the
Nazis. There were mixed results for those Kolniczanski's who equated
survival with flight; some survived while others did not.

The testimony of Adam Frydman was essential in understanding what
happened to the Kolniczanski's of Warsaw. He was sixteen years old when
the war started. The Frydman and Kolniczanski families were related by
marriage. His mother's sister, Fela, married Anchel Kolniczanski. He was
a frequent visitor to their apartment at 5 Ogrodowa Street, especially in
the years 1935-39 when Adam was attending the Nathanson Mechanical
College at 26 Graybowska Street, which was nearby. Adam spent many
hours at the apartment, doing his homework. By that point, Anchel's
children Lola, Gita and Marysia had all married. One child, Adek, still
lived at home.

Adam Frydman, 1997

In part, his testimony was the result of my relentless questioning. An obvious question that I felt I needed to ask was: Why did most family members remain in Warsaw prior to and during the German advance to the city? Family members had initially fled Warsaw on September 7, 1939. As Adam explained, they did this so as "not to be taken by the German army advancing to Warsaw." They were part of a mass flight described as a "spontaneous, panicked escape of civilians with no clear destination in mind."[172] Bronek Hermelin, the husband of Anchel's daughter, Marysia, was one of these; he escaped Warsaw and reached the United States. Other family members who had fled (Anchel, his son Adek and others) eventually returned to Warsaw.

Adam explained why family members did not try to leave again. His answer was clear and to the point. "We were all (almost) financially able to do it. We had relations in Western countries, Australia, U.S.A., and very close at that. I think that the attachment to the very large family mainly in Warsaw, the properties, business all this was a handicap. In the Kolniczanski's case, (Anchel), there was his involvement in the meat business, four children, two married, one divorced, they weren't young anymore. Fela and Anchel were well over 50." Nonetheless, some relatives chose flight. The granddaughter of Icie Kolniczanski, spoke in an interview about leaving Warsaw in the fall of 1939. Rivka Zen discussed how her grandparents left Warsaw with the assistance of a former slaughterhouse worker. She and her mother, Eva, survived the war in Russia; Icie and Sura were shot while escaping Poland.

On the other hand, Bronek's wife, Marysia (Anchel's daughter) remained and eventually died in Warsaw. Adam described the chain of events that led to her death. She left the ghetto during the massive deportation of the Warsaw ghetto around July or August 1942 and settled on the Polish side. Until the 1943 uprising, she was able to maintain communication with the family. Where and how she left the ghetto is not known. Given the fact that members of the Kolniczanski family lived on nearby streets, Marysia may have crossed over to the Polish side through

the Courts of Justice on 12-14 Ogrodowa Street, where an estimated
twenty to thirty thousand Jews escaped the ghetto. She would have needed
to acquire a special pass to enter the building and she would have had to
bribe various police officials who then would have allowed her to exit to
the Polish side. Adam had reason to believe she was denounced, arrested
and executed in public in either December 1943 or January 1944. The
procedure for a public execution was as follows:

> In all instances the course of proceedings followed a more or less
> identical pattern: strong police detachments arrived by car to the
> chosen place of execution, they stopped the traffic, cleared the
> street of all vehicles and pedestrians and put strong barriers at
> both ends of the street. They ordered that all gates, doors and
> windows in the area be closed and forbade anyone to leave the
> shops or approach the windows overlooking the street. The "clear-
> ing" of the area took only a few minutes to complete after which
> a column of motor-vehicles headed by the firing squad brought
> in the prisoners under heavy escort. Their hands were usually tied
> behind their backs, sometimes the victims were tied in pairs. At
> the earlier executions the prisoners were dressed in their ordi-
> nary clothes but later they were brought wearing only their un-
> der- clothes or special clothes made of paper sacking. Since the
> execution at which one of the Poles facing the firing squad had
> shouted "Long live Poland," the prisoners were brought gagged
> with rag swabs or gypsum paste with adhesive plaster stuck across
> their mouths to prevent such outbursts of patriotic feelings. On
> certain occasions the prisoners' eyes were bound or they were
> made to put paper bags over their heads before being stood against
> the wall. They were shot at by volleys of machine-gun fire in groups
> of 5 to 10 at a time. At the end of the execution an officer checked
> whether all were dead by kicking the bodies and finished off the
> wounded with pistol shot. Then the bodies would be loaded onto
> a lorry and taken to the former Ghetto. The place of execution
> would be immediately cleared away, the pavement flushed with
> water from a hose and detachments of Jews from the labour camp
> in Gesia Street would scrub off the blood stains. When order was
> restored the police vans drove away and everything returned to
> normal. But often even before the Nazis moved away people would
> rush to the place of execution...[173]

Since she was executed after November 1943, her name appeared on
a poster.

> In November 1943 the Gestapo thought up still more convincing
> means to remind the public that they were ruled by terrorism.

	Date and place of execution	Date and medium of announcement	Announ[ced] number [of] victim[s]
10	12. XI. 1943 Nowy Świat Street	13. XI. 1943 poster	60
11	12. XI. 1943 Kępna Street	13. XI. 1943 „	
12	17. XII. 1943 Warsaw-West rail-way station	18. XI. 1943 „	43
13	17. XI. 1943 Białołęcka Street	18. XI. 1943 „	
14	24. XI. 1943 Nabielaka Street	25. XI. 1943 „	27
15	24. XI. 1943 Radzymińska Street	25. XI. 1943 „	
16	30. XI. 1943 Solec Street	30. XI. 1943 „	34
17	2. XII. 1943 Nowy Świat Street, 68	2. XII. 1943 „	34
18	3. XII. 1943 Puławska Street, 13	3. XII. 1943 „	100
19	3. XII. 1943 Puławska Street, 21/23	3. XII. 1943 „	
20	11. XII. 1943 Leszno Street	15. XII. 1943 „	270
21	14. XII. 1943 Theatre Place	15. XII. 1943 „	
22	18. XII. 1943 Wolska Street	20. XII. 1943 „	23
23	21. XII. 1943 Wolska Street	20. XII. 1943 ..	
24	23. XII. 1943 Górczewska Street	27. XII. 1943 ..	43
25	31. XII. 1943 Towarowa Street	3. I. 1944 „	43
26	13. I. 1944 Górczewska Street	14. I. 1944 „	200
27	24. I. 1944 Kiliński Street	26. I. 1944 „	50
23	28. I. 1944 Jerozolimskie Avenue	29. I. 1944 • „	102
29	2. II. 1944 Ujazdowskie Avenue	2. II. 1944 „	100

LIST OF PUBLIC EXECUTIONS WHICH TOOK PLACE
ON THE STREETS OF WARSAW
from 16. X. 1943 to 15. II. 1944

Date and place of execution		Date and medium of announcement		Announced number of victims
16. X. 1943	Madaliński Street	16. X. 1943	mega-phone	20
17. X. 1943	Piękna Street	18. X. 1943	,,	20
20. X. 1943	Warsaw-Gdańsk rail-way station	20. X. 1943	,,	20
22. X. 1943	Młynarska Street	22. X. 1943	,,	10
23. X. 1943	Miedzeszyn Embankment	24. X. 1943	,,	20
26. X. 1943	Leszno Street	27. X. 1943	,,	30
30. X. 1943	Towarowa Street	31. X. 1943	,,	10
9. XI. 1943	Wawelska Street	10. XI. 1943	poster	
9. XI. 1943	Płocka Street	13. XI. 1943	,,	40

The names of those executed were no longer announced by street megaphone, instead large posters were printed on bright red paper bearing the names of those already executed. . .[174]

According to the list of public executions, she may have been shot in any of the following locations:[175] She was in her early thirties at the time of her execution. How ironic that her Hebrew name means "sea of bitterness or sorrow," [176] which in many ways is an accurate summary of her life underground and her death.

Given the nature of this research, it is not surprising that no trace in the form of documents or testimony was found on some of the Kolniczanski's. This was the case with Shifra (nee Kolniczanski) Schnichter. Her only son, Henry, was one of only a few Kolniczanski descendants to survive. The details add up to a mystery. Adam met Henry a number of times in the years 1946 and 1948. Henry was living then in the Hotel Polonia. The Hotel Polonia was one of the few buildings in the center of Warsaw that had not been destroyed, and for an obvious rea-

Henry Schichter, 1949

son: the Nazis used the hotel during their occupation of the city. Somehow, during the war, Henry managed to flee Warsaw and reach Romania. He spoke at length about how he survived the sinking of the Struma. Henry maintains he reached Turkish waters. This is puzzling, given the fact that the many accounts of the Struma sinking identify only one survivor, David Stoliar. Other accounts from relatives also refer to Henry having been a passenger on this ship. Also mysterious is the account from several relatives that he was arrested in 1949 (we do not know why) and later died in prison.

Other Kolniczanski's who did not survive the war, remained trapped in the Warsaw ghetto. One indication of how dramatically their lives had changed was what happened to the Praga slaughterhouse. As of late fall 1939, it was "closed to Jewish workers who had been a large part of its personnel."[177]

The Praga slaughterhouse had been so much a part of the Kolniczanski's economic identity. Its closing had the profound impact of undermining the family's means of support. Like so many other families, they would fall back on savings, which were strictly controlled by the Germans: "Banks were allowed to pay out to Jews a maximum of 250 zlotys a week from their accounts. A Jewish family was allowed to keep a maximum of 2,000 zlotys in cash outside of banking institutions." [178]

The family was spared the trauma of moving into the ghetto because the apartment was located within the ghetto boundaries. In a sense, they were "lucky," because they did not have to face the hardships endured by residents of other sections of Warsaw and refugees.

There is no doubt that the Kolniczanski family was aware of and exposed to the visible anti-Semitic incidents so much a part of ghetto life. One incident serves to illustrate this, which took place on 2 Ogrodowa Street at the start of the German occupation of Warsaw. "As soup and bread were distributed to local residents, shouts of 'Jude' were heard directed at some people standing in line. Many Jews were identified and thrown out of the line, denied the soup and bread." [179] While the vast majority of ghetto residents struggled to secure food to eat, there were a select few who dined in the new cafes, one which existed "...on Ogrodowa Street a garden cafe, called 'Bajka' (fairy tale) ...The tables are outside; there is a little grass and two trees." [180]

The sector between Chlodna and Elektoralna streets; the gate was then situated just at the corner of Elektoralna and Solna streets. Seen in the background is a house with a decorative element in the form of a small tower dominating its roof. Another house with a similar element is seen, further in the background, situated at the corner of Solna and Ogrodowa streets. Between these towers was situated the butcher's shop of my ancestors at 9 Solna Street.

Ogrodowa was like so many other streets, the site of unplanned and planned violent murders: "...a Jewish woman, Opatowska, was murdered at 7 Ogrodowa Street."[181] That address was the former residence of Icie Kolniczanski and his family.

Any incident was an excuse to single out and murder at random: "High numbers of dead at 29 Ogrodowa Street. The remaining occupants were taken out, no notice was taken of their papers. The cause — a piece of glass fell on the street when there were Germans passing."[182]

I can only wonder what went through the minds of family members at this time, perhaps, given historical precedents, the Kolniczanski's believed this was another occupier who would eventually leave and things would return to normal. All they had to do was weather the storm and it would pass. Confiscation of property and the eventual ghettoization must have seemed like a repeat of the past. What was a new and foreboding sign was the ongoing struggle to secure food to eat.

Front L to R, Guta, Fela and Marysia
Back L to R, Adek, Lola

With an official daily allowance of 184 calories[183], it was obvious that in a short time, the Kolniczanski family, like others trapped in the ghetto would die of starvation. Survival meant only one thing: the smuggling of food. The Kolniczanski's family involvement with smuggling was made possible due to contact they had established in the meat trade before the war. "The big operators were for the most part former merchants and factory owners in the food industry — flour dealers, bakers, slaughterhouse operators."[184]

There were five ways that the Kolniczanski's and other smugglers brought food into the ghetto: "across the walls, at the exit points, through underground tunnels, through the sewers and the houses on the borderline." [185]

To smuggle meat took a degree of inventiveness: "Specially constructed mobile ramps were set against the walls on both sides to smuggle over live cows and oxen." [186] Anchel was directly involved in smuggling meat of all kinds, including horse meat. In addition to its role in meat smuggling, the meat shop at 9 Solna Street served other purposes. Very often, there was nothing to sell, but the shop became a hiding place for family members in an effort to escape Gestapo and SS roundups. It was common to lock up the shop with padlocks and spend the night there in order not to be taken away.

The meat shop remained open for business from 1939-1942. Its purpose shifted from selling meat in the pre-war and early period of the German occupation to assisting in the smuggling of meat. Fela's role in meat smuggling would become more prominent in the years that followed, In early 1942, Fela sublet part of the shop to a family engaged in the sale of delicatessan and dairy goods also smuggled into the ghetto.

The Kolniczanski's, like so many other families, were forced to confront the breakdown of essential services that would have limited the spread of typhus. During an epidemic, Anchel contracted the disease. I took some comfort in the knowledge that after so many years, Anchel's fate was now at least known by the family, thanks to the testimony of Adam Frydman. Anchel was one of 15,449 cases of typhus in 1941. "It begins with a rapid rise in temperature, chills, a feeling of impending doom, weakness, pain in the limbs and severe headache. On about the fourth or fifth day, a rash appears on the skin, usually on the shoulders, chest and back. It then spreads to the arms and legs, the backs of the hands and feet and sometimes the soles; rarely does it appear on the face." [187]

His contraction of and death from typhus clearly demonstrates the sharp contrast between how the family had lived before the Holocaust and how they were forced to live during it, and it underscores the difference between power and powerlessness.

What was most sad in light of all that I have learned from archival and testimony sources was the shocking contrast between his past and present. Typhus had effectively reduced this powerful, assertive individual to a broken, sick, bed-ridden man. His sickness and death must have produced a shocking effect on his relatives, for he represented the most influential and well-known member of the Kolniczanski family. His death must have made other family members painfully aware of their own dire predicaments.

Anchel died of typhus in October 1941. It was a period that saw a rapid increase in typhus cases. He contracted typhus during a raging epidemic, in the second half of 1941. [188] Adam described it as "one of the hardest periods in the life of the ghetto."

After hunger, typhus was the second problem utmost in the minds of ghetto residents. As of August, one historian of the ghetto estimated there were "about 7,000 typhus patients under treatment in their apartments and 9,000 in ghetto hospitals." [189] The raging typhus epidemic and hunger that gripped the ghetto in 1941 meant that many victims were found on the street. "The most beloved were stripped of their tattered but still serviceable clothing and laid out marked on the sidewalks to await the morning burial wagon." [190] Anchel stayed at home and was not sent to the so-called hospital where typhus victims were housed and left to die. He had the luxury of dying in his apartment and was buried in the Jewish Cemetary. The task of burying relatives was filled with danger. German soldiers could very easily notice a funeral procession, resulting in the marchers' capture or execution.

In spite of all my efforts during a 1996 visit to Warsaw and afterwards through correspondence, I could not locate any records of Anchel's burial. But unlike so many others whose bodies were deposited on ghetto streets, Anchel did have the benefit of a burial, an indication that the Kolniczanski's still had sufficient material resources, though limited, that allowed for a private burial.

I was fortunate to obtain some information[191] on 5 Ogrodowa, Anchel's residence, during the ghetto period. The apartment house typically had apartments with 5 rooms. In the front of the building was a square, fenced courtyard with trees in the middle. Before the war, residents rarely interacted. This changed during and after the seizure of Warsaw. During ghettoization, the building became very crowded. Refugees arrived in great numbers. Everyday, the Nazis raided apartments, taking various possessions, furniture, jewelry and silverware.

Like so many other buildings, 5 Ogrodowa had a house committee. These tenant committees provided a vast array of services and functions. During the typhus outbreaks, the committee at 5 Ogrodowa made a concerted effort to collect food from tenants to assist those infected with typhus. During the epidemic, the Nazi procedure (which changed over time) was to close down the building for two weeks. Those infected were sent to various bath houses for so-called treatment. But this did not always occur, such as in Anchel's case. Many victims were confined to their apartments. Family members did what they could to cope with the uncertainty and terror of everyday life in the ghetto. In the case of Anchel's son, Adek, this meant becoming a member Judische Ordnungsdienst or the Warsaw Jewish Ghetto Police, Second Reserve Unit, Badge Number 1266.[192]

Adek had to satisfy eligibility requirements and go through the following process. Candidates had to

> be twenty-one to forty years of age, have a diploma from a Gymnasium, be of proper height and weight, have completed military service, have an unblemished past and be recommended by two persons. Each candidate had to pass the screening of three of four offices: the so-called small commissions that collected all necessary personal documents, a medical commission and lastly the

List of Auxiliary Ghetto Police Members

"super scrutiny" commission, presided over by the commandant
of the ghetto police. [193]

As a member of the reserve, his duties were administrative and involved record-keeping. At first, he was on Grzybowska Street, the former
residence of the Nozyk synagogue. As of 1941, the reserve was housed in
the order headquarters at 17 Ogrodowa Street, very close to his residence
on 5 Ogrodowa Street.

My concern, of course, is what were Adek's motives for joining. There
were benefits to joining, such as ". . .immunity to deportation to labor
camps or abduction off the streets."[194] He had to have been aware of the
all-too-common incidents of terror and murder, which occurred on his
street. "When the Gestapo sent for a certain Jewish merchant of Warsaw
who lived in Ogrodowa Street, he jumped out of the window of his home

and was killed."[195] The most disturbing question is his possible role in the summer and fall deportations of 1942. Adam's testimony provides the reassuring answer to my concern: no role whatsoever. In fact, during the first weeks of the deportation action, Adam, his father, brother, Morris, and sometimes Adek used the shop as a hiding place. "To avoid being taken, we slept in the shop, windows covered and locked from outside."

There is no doubt family members could see the daily movement and participation of the Jewish police in the deportations.

> "Every morning from our window, which looked out on Ogrodowa we watched the Jewish police assemble in front of their headquarters. Armed with clubs, they were divided into two groups. One marched out of the police yard through a gate into Leszno in the greater ghetto. The second went through Ogrodowa in the direction of the Zhelasna bridge to the small ghetto. So began each day's bloody chase." [196]

As of August 15, the Kolniczanski's who lived at 5 Ogrodowa Street were marked for deportation. [197] Not far from 5 Ogrodowa, roundups of Jews were underway as of July 31st: "about 2,000 people had been removed from the buildings at 27, 29, 31 Ogrodowa Street." [198]

Their survival and that of the Frydman family during the summer and fall deportations was the result of their finding various hiding places and never remaining in any one place for too long for fear of discovery. Adam identifies various addresses used during and after the mass deportations, "the remainder of the family moved to Plac Muranowski 11 then to Zamenhofa 38." There is this description of the bunker:

> .. This underground shelter is well-equipped, almost, one might say, with all conveniences: electric light, gas, running water (plus water stocks and their own private well), waste disposal and essential food stocks including flour, vegetables, syrup, dried bread and potatoes. In case the electricity and gas is cut off, they also have stocks of charcoal, paraffin lamps and candles. [199]

As was the case with other bunkers, this one was well-hidden "...beneath a bombed-out ruin. From the outside, one can see a pile of bricks and rubble." [200]

From archival and secondary sources, I determined that Yoskie and his sons escaped the summer deportations. Two facts can be established: that Yoskie was a prisoner at Pawiak and that certain circumstances surrounded his execution. In a recent work on the Pawiak Prison, the authors identified a list of prisoners. One (misspelled) named on that list

432	Aneksy			
1	2	3	4	5
87	Ichzelbst	fryzjer	Warszawa, ul. Freta	
88	Igelberg	mechanik	Warszawa, ul. Hoża	
89	Ilitowicz	—	Warszawa	
90	Jakubowicz	—	Łódź	
91	Jas	—	Rembertów	
92	Kaczmarek	—	Poznań	
93	Kadysiewicz	—	Warszawa-Praga	
94	Kahan	—	Warszawa	
95	Kanarek	handel zbożem	Pułtusk	
96	Kapitulnik	—	Toruń	
97	Kaplan	skład zboża	Warszawa, ul. Grzybowska	
98	Kaplan	—	Warszawa, ul. Gęsia 39	
99	Karaś	—	—	
100	Klinger	adwokat	Warszawa	
101	Klotz	krawiec	Kraków	
→ 102	Kolczewski	rzeźnik	Warszawa	
103	Kopelman	—	Warszawa	
104	Kordowski	profesor	Wilno	
105	Korolczyk	kowal	Nowy Dwór	

Pawiak prisoner list with a misspelled reference to a Kolniczanski.

appears as Kolczewski. [201] The occupation next to the name is rzeznik, in English, this means butcher. Anchel and Motke were identified as butcher in the Polish business directory of 1929, indicating that the butcher label was also applicable to Yoskie. Many inmates of Pawiak were caught in the Polish sector. If Yoskie and his family had fled to the Polish side, it is certain that they lived in constant fear of exposure. Arrest could result from bands of "schmalzoyniks," the name given to young blackmailers found roaming the streets in search of Jews who had crossed over. Other blackmailers searched for Jews in apartment buildings. In addition, there were a fair share of uniformed and undercover police agents who also searched for Jews.

Joskie and his family were well-off, which made it possible for them to cross over, bringing with them foreign currency and valuables. Like the majority of Jews who crossed over, they lived underground, confronted with the daily challenge of evading detection and capture.

One of Yoskie's sons, Jacob, survived until January 18, 1943. Adam provided important information on Jacob, who was a frequent visitor to Anchel's home. He was an electrical engineering student in a Technical College at Stawki Street. He also was politically active in a right-wing Zionist group known as Betar.

On January 18, 1943, the final effort to liquidate the remaining Jews of the ghetto began. Adam's sister, Hanka, provided information on Jacob, including his participation in the "little uprising" of Janury 18. The fact that Jacob (also known as Kuba) was actively involved with Betar sheds light on his role in the small uprising.

Formed as the youth organization of the Zionist Revisionist party, Betar had one aim: to establish a Jewish state by any means necessary including military means. Betar was unique among Jewish organizations at that time in that it advocated military training. The various Betar units or branches formed "military service units which were trained in the use of firearms, mainly rifles." [202] This fact is useful in explaining not only Jacob's training as a member of Betar, but also his participation in the small uprising. Of all the Jewish resistance organizations in the Warsaw ghetto, "Betar was one of the first — if not the first — youth organization that began rallying its forces to relieve the sense of internal isolation that prevailed, and to prepare for the danger that threatened the people as a whole from outside." [203]

Training meant leaving one's family, placing oneself completely under the command of the organization, just like a soldier in an army. It also meant living underground and working on clandestine activities. The idea of armed resistance to the Germans started in 1940 when the first ZZW resistance cells were formed. At the time of its formation, the ZZW consisted of ex-soldiers, groups of partisans, some leftist elements and members of Betar.

In Adam's October 1996 letter, he described Jacob's participation and death in the January 18th uprising: "...one of the groups he was leading fought a battle at Mila Street, No. 2." The military structure of the ZZW sheds light on Jacob's role in the January 18, 1943 revolt. In the years 1940-41, the military organization of ZZW altered the structure of its fighting units. In 1940, there were "five-man sections, each consisting of four fighters and a section commander; two such sections formed a squad."[204] As of 1941, there was a change, in that ". . .the squads were enlarged to include three sections, one of them armed with automatic weapons." [205] What this probably means is that at the time of the revolt, Jacob was likely in command of a squad consisting of at least 12 armed fighters.

Frydman's letter stated further that during that battle, "Some of the SS members were killed and Kuba was also a victim of this battle." Hanka's involvement with the Jewish underground as a courier lends credence to the statements she made to Adam. Whether or not Jacob fought as a member of ZZW is at best an educated guess, derived from his membership in Betar. Another possibility is that he fought on that day in a group of "Wildcats." These Wildcats escaped the Selektion. Wildcats were known to be in hiding on Mila Street during the first act of resistance of January 18: "Then they march off to Mila Street and surround apartments where railroad workers of the Ostbahn live together with the Wild ones." [206] Since he and other members of the Kolniczanski family survived the deportations, there is no doubt that they went and remained in hiding and Jacob may have fought in a Wildcat group.

The year of 1943 was a fateful one for some members of the Kolniczanski family. Jacob's death in January was followed by the murder of Anchel's son Adek. He was caught and shot in a summary execution by the German SS on February 1943. Given the fact that he was shot in February, it is likely that his place of execution was the notorious

LIST OF EXECUTIONS OF WARSAW RESIDENTS

Data	Place	Number of killed
7 July 1942	Wood in Moczydło and Dąbrówka district	640(?)
17 July 1942	Ghetto	ca 40
22—23 July 1942	Ghetto	ca 20
5—6 August 1942	Ghetto	52
19—20 August 1942	Ghetto	ca 20
15 August 1942	Okęcie	5
July-September 1942	Ghetto	5961
Summer 1942 (?)	Laski	21
Summer 1942 (?)	Laski	23
Summer 1942 (or Spring 1943)	Laski	61
Autumn 1942	Laski	50
3 September 1942	not traced	dozens
24 September 1942	not traced	14
15 October 1942	Łuże dunes	39
16 October 1942	Rembertów	10
16 October 1942	Toruńska Street	10
16 October 1942	Mszczonowska Street	10
16 October 1942	Szczęśliwice	10
16 October 1942	Marki	10
28—29 October 1942	Kabaty Wood	dozens
October-November(?) 1942	Łuże dunes	18
1 December 1942	Vicinity of the Pawiak	8
8/9 December 1942	not traced	27
1942 (?)	Łuże dunes	28
6 January 1943	Chojnów Wood	20
18 January 1943	not traced (near Łomiar ')	5
January 1943	Ghetto	1171
2 February 1943	Chojnów Wood	19
12 February 1943	Chojnów Wood	70
23 February 1943	not traced	19
10 March 1943	Pawiak	dozens
13 March 1943	Ghetto	ca 210

Chojnow Wood—outside Warsaw. [207] Survival for the remaining members of the family meant an existence in underground bunkers. During this time, Adam was separated from his sister Hanka, and the remaining members of the Kolniczanski family, who lived in these bunkers during most of the large uprising of April 19, 1943. Hanka, Fela, Lola, Gita and her daughter Anna, were forced out of their Zamenhofa Street bunker on May 8, 1943. Adam was in another bunker with his father and brother. According to the Stroop report for May 8: "A total of 1,091 Jews were apprehended in the bunkers today..."[208] They met at the notorious Umschlagplatz (assembly point) on the night of May 8th and remained there on May 9. The Kolniczanski's and Frydman were placed on the May 10, 1943 transport to the usual final destination—Treblinka. One incomplete count of the number on the May 10 transport states: "...deported 875 male and unknown number of female and children from the Warsaw ghetto."[209] As fate would have it, and for reasons unknown, out of a transport of 3,500 people, 400, including the Kolniczanski's and Frydman, were rerouted to Majdanek, which appeared at first, to be a reprieve from certain death at the Treblinka killing center. But Majdanek eventually would prove otherwise. Upon arrival in Lublin, they were marched the 3 km to Majdanek. The two families reunited at the unloading ramp.

Of the 40,000 Jews deported to Majdanek during late April and early May, 16,000 were from Warsaw. [210] During that period when the Kolniczanski's and Frydman's arrived there, extermination was the end for "over 50 percent of the new arrivals."[211] Another account notes: "Mass gassing reached its height from May to July 1943, when thousands of Jews brought from the Warsaw ghetto were executed."[212] Adam and Hanka survived Majdanek and bore witness to the extermination of the Kolniczanski's. The extermination procedure at Majdanek has been described in great detail:

> The procedure was the following: After a Jewish transport had arrived, it was isolated in an empty yard surrounded with barbed wire, next to the bath and the gas chamber situated in the same building...There the Jews would spend the first night in the open air. In the morning, Florstedt assisted by Thuman (head of the prisoner division) and the crematorium's chief Muhsfedt, started the selection of prisoners. The healthy and the young ones were sent to the bath. The old and weak and the children were directed to the Other Room, seemingly furnished like a bath, which actually was a gas chamber...[213]

From comments Hanka made to Adam, I learned what happened to

Fela, Lola, Gita and her 9 year-old daughter, Anna. Anna had been selected for gassing. Fela and her daughters refused to be separated from
her.

This was one of the most disturbing and upsetting facts I learned
about the fates of relatives. I can never expect to fully understand the
sheer terror they must have felt as they realized their final end. Their
refusal to be separated from 9 year-old Anna is, without a doubt, evidence of how close this family was. Confronted with the horrible choice
of only some of them surviving, or all of them dying, the family chose to
remain together. They died as a family. The selection of Anna leaves no
doubt as to the scope of the Nazi intent to biologically destroy the Jews.

Anna was "one of the 100,000 out of 400,000 residents of the ghetto
who were under 15 years old. . ." [214] When the war began, she was five
years old, the age when she should have been starting elementary school.

"As soon as the war started, Jewish children in Warsaw lost their
schools." [215] Even with the reestablishment of elementary schooling in
spring 1941, classroom instruction was substandard. The difficulties of
schooling Jewish children imposed by the Nazis represented one of a series of incremental steps leading toward the mental and physical destruction of Jewish children, the future of the Jewish people.

Desperate efforts were made by ghetto residents to fight off hunger,
the most vulnerable among them were the children: "starvation was reap-
ing its biggest harvest among children since they were the least resistant
to suffering and hardship. They succumbed to many diseases brought
about by improper nourishment." [216] While children were considered to
be the weakest group in the ghetto, they were called upon to do extraordinary feats, such as begging and smuggling. Despite the fact that Anna
was from a well-to-do family, she could not escape the daily horror of the
street and the lack of a normal childhood.

There was no escape from the overcrowding, lack of sanitation, the
sight of dead bodies, beggars and Jews abused by the Germans. With these
sights, it was no wonder that ghetto children were no longer afraid of
death. The boundary lines between life and death for these children became blurred, when one considers this example: "In one courtyard the
children played a game, tickling a corpse." [217] It also was a sad fact that
the earliest victims of the July 22, 1942 deportations were children.

I have been able to piece together the circumstances of Yoskie
Kolniczanski's death. It has been established with some degree of certainty that he was a prisoner at Pawiak. There were questions which I
found answers for, such as, what did he spend his time doing, when and
how was he killed, and who had direct responsibility for his death. An

archival file at Yad Vashem and secondary references provided the answers to these questions. The date and means of his execution can be pinpointed with some degree of certainty. Joskie was most likely killed in July 1944. A Warsaw ghetto file obtained from Yad Vashem contains a list of 40 persons executed in July 1944. The name Kolniczanski appears and the spelling is correct except for a missing "ni." The occupation listed is

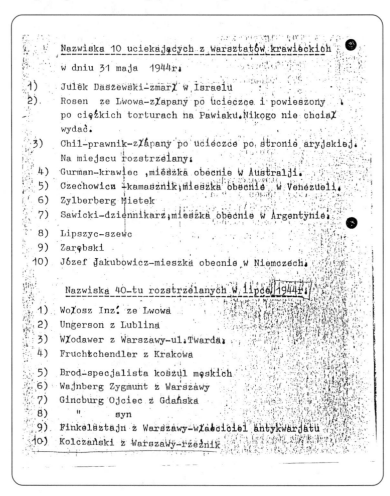

Nazwiska 10 uciekających z warsztatów krawieckich

w dniu 31 maja 1944r.

1)   Julek Daszewski-zmarł w Israelu
2)   Rosen ze Lwowa-złapany po ucieczce i powieszony
     po ciężkich torturach na Pawiaku.Nikogo nie chciał
     wydać.
3)   Chil-prawnik-złapany po ucieczce po stronie aryjskiej.
     Na miejscu rozstrzelany.
4)   Gurman-krawiec ,mieszka obecnie w Australji.
5)   Czechowicz -kamasznik,mieszka obecnie w Venezueli.
6)   Zylberberg Mietek
7)   Sawicki-dziennikarz,mieszka obecnie w Argentynie.
8)   Lipszyc-szewc
9)   Zarębski
10) Józef Jakubowicz-mieszka obecnie w Niemczech.

Nazwiska 40-tu rozstrzelanych w lipcu 1944r.

1)   Wołosz Inż. ze Lwowa
2)   Ungerson z Lublina
3)   Włodawer z Warszawy-ul.Twarda.
4)   Fruchtchendler z Krakowa

5)   Brod-specjalista koszul męskich
6)   Wajnberg Zygmunt z Warszawy
7)   Gincburg Ojciec z Gdańska
8)   "   syn
9)   Finkelsztajn z Warszawy-właściciel antykwarjatu
10) Kolczański z Warszawy-rzeźnik

butcher. [218]

In a secondary source, I came across the following reference: "...on July 14, 42 Jewish prisoners employed in the workshops were murdered by a warden, Engelberth Fruhwirth." [219] Another secondary source provides the following: "...they selected for execution the forty from the group of Jewish workmen and spared the true artisans, whom they still needed." [220] The author, who escaped from Pawiak, had this to say, "when I escaped from Pawiak with the ten men on May 30, 1944, another one hundred eighty-two men and women remained in the Jewish work group in prison. Of that number, forty-two men were shot on July 14th." [221]

Two sources confirm the date and number of Pawiak prisoners executed. A reason for the executions also can be explained.

> Now the German front collapsed outside Lublin. The Russian Army, in its race toward Warsaw, was pressing westward with overwhelming force. The Germans lost their heads; they knew they had to get out of Warsaw. So they carried out the final and bloodiest massacre of Pawiak prisoners. Unerringly, they selected for execution the forty from the group of Jewish workmen. [222]

It was in July 1944 that the Soviet Army was advancing toward Lublin, another confirmation of the date of the executions. Names of the forty-two persons executed appears on another list [223]

Data	Place	Number of killed
9 June 1944	Ghetto	10—20 (?)
9–10 June 1944	Ghetto	over 100
16 June 1944	Ghetto	ca 75
19 June 1944	not traced	ca 80
20 June 1944	Ghetto	ca 20
21 June 1944	Ghetto	ca 75
27 June 1944	Ghetto	dozens
7 July 1944	Ghetto	37
10—11 July 1944	Ghetto	36
14 July 1944	Ghetto	42
20—21 July 1944	Ghetto	173
26 July 1944	Ghetto	dozens (?)
31 July 1944	Pawiak hospital	ca 10
1939—1944	Młochów Forest nr. Nadarzyn	150 *

I suspect Yoskie survived in Pawiak until July 1944 because he belonged to a select group of Jewish artisans, a slave labor force useful to
the Germans. Prior to the annihilation of the Waraw ghetto, there was "a
group of about a hundred to a hundred and fifty Jewish artisans. . ."[224].
They were executed in May 1943. Another group was formed, meaning it
is possible that Yoskie then became a member of this group. Forty of
them were executed in July 1944.

As I researched the fate of the other Kolniczanski's, identification of
a perpetrator who was directly responsible, and who saw family members killed could not be located. But in the case of Yoskie's execution, I
was able to acquire facts on the perpetrator, Engelberth Fruhwirth. He
was born in 1902, and had the rank of SS Unterscharfuhrer.[225] His reputation among the prisoners was someone "whose brutality was a byword
in the Pawiak..."[226] He was at one time a waiter in Vienna.[227] His Austrian
Nazi origins speak volumes as to a fanatical hatred directed at the Jews. A
former prisoner of Pawiak made many references to his hatred of the
Jews at the prison: ". . .in all that time, treatment of the Jews did not
change. The Ukrainians as a group no longer tortured us, but the Austrian Fruhwirth did not stop until the last moment."[228] In all passages, he
is characterized as heartless and cruel. His main target for his brutality
always was the Jews: "The Jews as always, were the chief victims."[229] A
precise portrait of Fruhwirth appears in the account of another prisoner
who survived Pawiak.

> The supervisor (Oberwachmajster) Engelberth Fruhwirth origi-
> nally from Vienna, occupation waiter, was well known at the
> Pawiak prison, as a "shouter." During working time, he was well-
> known to roam around in Pawiak, pushed himself everywhere,
> and because of his 'important' post in the prison, substituting for
> the commander of the prison, he acted with exaggerated pride,
> and therefore was called "general." He often came into the work-
> shops where he took a liking to the prisoners who worked there.
> The general had an effect on the prisoners. Everyone rushed to
> do any sort of work. Woe! to the one whom he would catch sit-
> ting idle or talking. Fruhwirth drove out the prisoners into the
> yard, and found for them various difficult works to do, or to do
> 'prison gymnastics.' For the smallest offense, he used punishment
> like placing people in 'Dunkelzelle' (dark cell), lashing or holding
> food packages back from prisoners. In later periods, packages were
> delivered to prisoners. He often took part in executions. Cooks in
> the kitchen were also afraid of Fruhwirth and prepared special
> food for him of better quality than for the commander of the
> prison, as being a waiter he was well familiar with cooking and

preparing foods. In spite of his 41 years of age, he was very concerned about his looks. He spent many hours at the men's hairdresser's where the barber performed the most sophisticated beautifying steps on him. [230]

Fruhwirth's direct role in the carrying out of executions is one of the most relevant aspects of the prisoner's portrait of him. I conclude that it was highly probable that he was directly responsible for the execution of Yoskie Kolniczanski. I can't help but wonder how much suffering and humiliation Yoskie Kolniczanski had to endure from Fruhwirth.

Saul Frydman, father of Adam, worked in the Warsaw Abbatoir as an accountant. He was involved with the Kolniczanski brothers in the meat business.

During the infamous mass shooting at Majdanek, which was the largest that occurred at any camp in a single day, the Erntefest or "harvest festival" in which 18,000 prisoners were shot, Adam's father was murdered. Adam survived Majdanek, enduring 7 weeks of horror. This was his comment on how he coped and survived: "To remain a human being in the darkest, macabre conditions was my personal aim. It was very easy to succumb into the pits of horror." On June 26, he was transported to a slave labor camp, Skarzysko-Kamienna.

The year 1944 was marked by the sad coincidence of the deaths of Yoskie and Robert. They were murdered five months apart, Robert in February 1944, Yoskie in July 1944. In both cases, they were killed just six months prior to the liberation of their respective cities, Warsaw and Paris. Warsaw was liberated in January 1945 by the Red Army. Paris was liberated by Free French Forces in August 1944.

After the war, a few men who had worked for the Kolniczanski's in the slaughterhouse came to visit my grandfather in New York, they told him that none of the Kolniczanski's had survived. My grandfather was visibly shaken and very saddened by the news. A few years after this incident, he would also learn what had happened to the Kolniczanski branch of the family in France.

Notes

[172] Yisrael Gutman, The Jews of Warsaw 1939-43, Bloomington: Indiana University Press, 1989, p. 4

[173] Szymon Datner, Janusz Gumkowski, Kazimierz Leszcynski Genocide 1939-45 (Warsaw: Interpress, 1962) pp. 116-117

[174] Ibid, p. 117

[175] Ibid, pp. 119-20

[176] Alfred Kolatch, Complete Dictionary of English and Hebrew First Names Jonathon David Publishers, New York: 1984, p. 371

[177] Bernard Goldstein, Five Years in the Warsaw Ghetto (New York: Viking Press, 1949) p. 44

[178] Gutman, p. 21

[179] Memoirs, Bulletin of Jewish Historical Institute, A. Lewin, p. 130, Warsaw: 1957)

[180] Mary Berg, Warsaw Ghetto, NY: L.B. Fisher, 1945, p. 61

[181] Ibid, p. 126

[182] Ibid, p. 139

[183] Gutman, p. 66

[184] Goldstein, Five Years p. 80

[185] Emanuel Ringelblum, Polish Jewish Relations, New York: Howard Fertig, 1976, p. 85

[186] Goldstein, Five Years p. 80

[187] Charles Roland, Courage Under Siege: Starvation, Disease and Death in the Warsaw Ghetto (New York: Oxford Press, 1992) p. 123

[188] Roland, p. 132

[189] Emanuel Ringelblum, Notes From the Warsaw Ghetto (NY: Shocken Books, 1958) p. 194

[190] Goldstein, Five Years p. 82

[191] Telephone interview with Barbara Urbanska-Yeager. her mother lived at 5 Ogrodowa Street during ghettoization and kept a detailed diary.

[192] I am thankful to Yale Reisner of the Ronald Lauder Foundation Genealogy Project at the Jewish Historical Institute of Poland for locating this document.

[193] Isaiah Trunk, Judenrat, University of Nebraska Press, 1996, p. 489

[194] Gutman, p. 86

[195] Arno Lustiger, ed. The Black Book of Polish Jewry (Germany: Syndikat

Buchgeseleschaft, 1995) p. 18

[196]Goldstein, Five Years, pp. 119-120

[197]Lustiger, p. 163

[198]Abraham Lewin, A Cup of Tears London: Oxford University Press, 1989 p.

[199]Dr. Hillel Seidman, The Warsaw Ghetto Diaries, Targun Press, Michigan, 1997) p. 199

[200]Ibid, p. 198

[201]Czechowicz and Gurman, The Memoirs of Czechowicz and Gurman (Warsaw: 1993) p. 431

[202]Chaim Lazar, Muranowska 7, Massada-P.E.C. Press, Tel Aviv, 1966, p. 46

[203]Lazar, p. 141

[204]Ibid

[205] Ibid

[206]Seidman, p. 249

[207]Wladyslaw Bartoszewski, Warsaw Death Ring 1939-1944 (Warsaw: Interpress Press, 1968) p. 356

[208]Stroop Report (New York: Pantheon Books, 1979)

[209]Zofia Leszczynska Kronika oboza na Majdanku (Lublin: Wydawnictwo Lubelskie 1980) p. 163

[210]Marzalek, p. 68

[211]Marzalek, p. 137

[212]Bartoszewski, p. 326

[213]Marzalek, p. 40

[214]Roland, p. 174

[215]Joseph Kernish, ed., To Live With Honor and Die With Honor, Jerusalem: Yad Vashem, 1986, p. 372

[216]Ibid, p. 376

[217]Ringelblum, p. 174

[218]Warsaw Ghetto Archives, Yad Vashem, Jerusalem

[219] Bartoszewski, p. 326

[220]Julien Hirshaut Jewish Martyrs of Pawiak (New York: Holocaust Library, 1982) p. 155

[221]Ibid, p. 228

[222]Ibid, p. 155

[223]Bartoszewski, p. 360

[224]Hirshaut. p. 34

[225]Hirshaut. p. 341

[226]Ibid

[227]Ibid, pp. 73-74

[228]Ibid, p. 74

[229]Len Wanat <u>Za Murami Pawiaka</u> (Warsaw: Interpress, 1960) p. 45

[230]Wanat, p. 277

CHAPTER SEVEN

The Holocaust
France

I T ALL BEGAN in September 1939 when the war was declared. My mother and aunt were 14 years old. Every summer, their parents would take them from Paris to Contrexville, where they sold pocketbooks in the marketplace. When the war was declared, they had to leave Contrexville because of its proximity to the German border. The municipality ordered all non-residents to leave because they feared infiltration by the Fifth Column, so they took the train back to Paris.

Paris was, at the time, ". . .the third biggest Jewish community outside Warsaw and New York."[231] At that time, the number of Jews in Paris was 149,734[232], the 20th arrondissement, where the Kolnitchanski family lived, had the second highest concentration of Jews in the city.[233]

When the general mobilization was declared, my uncle David was called up for the French Army. When he came home on leave, what struck my mother the most was the condition of his uniform. It was soiled and there were a lot of buttons missing. It was a symbol of La Drole de Guerre, "the phony war."

By 1940, my grandparents started to have doubts about staying in Paris because the city was starting to experience air raids. The searing sound of the siren woke them up in the middle of the night, and they had to rush to the subway to seek shelter. They decided then to leave the city. My grandfather travelled first to Le Mans in search of an apartment and work. When he found one, my grandmother, mother and aunt followed. My Uncle Albert came later during the mass migration out of the capital. It has been described as "La Grand Peur," or "L'exodus," in which ". . .between one-fifth and a quarter of the population took to the roads." [234]

The apartment in Le Mans did not have all the comforts of home. It had no running water, no toilet and no kitchen. To cook and clean, they had to carry buckets of water up the stairs from the yard where there was a faucet. Each time, they carried the water upstairs, the landlord was always on the stairs, watching them.

The family stayed in Le Mans only a few months. They had to leave because of the rapid German advance. On the way to the railroad station, my grandfather remembered the German luger that he had left in the apartment. It was his memento from the battle of Verdun. He went back and threw it in the river.

They caught the last train out of Le Mans. My mother related to me an incident that occurred on the train. There were eight people in the compartment. My grandfather was dozing, his beret, which he never went anywhere without, was next to him on the seat. It was a long ride and the train stopped constantly, it seemed. Suddenly, a sound like a gunshot broke the monotony. My grandfather was awakened with a start. He grabbed his beret and shouted, "Let's get out of here!" At that moment, they realized what the commotion was about. It was a cork that had popped out of a cider bottle on the baggage rack. Now it seems comical, but at the time, it illustrated how much tension and anxiety existed on that trip.

The trip took three days. The train stopped in La Rochelle and could go no further because of the impending advance of the Germans. The French blew up all the boats in order to block the harbor, so that they wouldn't fall into enemy hands.

Upon the train's arrival in La Rochelle, all the refugees were sheltered in a school. They slept on straw on the floor. For my mother, who was fifteen at the time, it was an exciting adventure. The war had not yet touched her life.

A few days later, the Germans arrived in La Rochelle. My mother could not completely describe how she felt when she witnessed the arrival of the first German column. It left her with a sense of intimidation, curiousity and fear, especially when she saw the advance column arriving in motorcycles and the officers riding behind them in the cars with swastika flags. They had an air of arrogance and triumph about them, looking down on the vanquished. It gave my mother an uneasy feeling to see it, but she never could have imagined what lay ahead.

The Armistice was signed in June 1940; it divided France into the Free and Occupied zones. There seemed to be no point in remaining in La Rochelle, so the family returned to Paris.

The Germans had arrived earlier in the area where the 20e ends, the Porte des Lilas, very near to where the family lived. There is this account of the atmosphere and attitudes of those witnessing the German army's arrival: "Il y avait du monde sur les troittoirs et je les regardais passer, anime a la fois d'un sentiment de curiosite et de crainte."[235] (There were a lot of people on the sidewalk and I was watching them pass by, animated at the time with a sentiment of curiosity and fear.)

There is this description of the German troops arriving and marching through various neighborhoods. "From Belleville to Pigalle, from Menilmontant to the Champs-Elysees, officers and men of the German forces were everywhere ceaselessly accosted by passers-by of all classes, who joked with the enemy, and offered them any kind of help they wanted."[236]

From 1940-1942, the family remained in Paris, each of them doing their best to cope with the German occupation. Like so many other Parisian Jews, the family had to register with the police. Family members gave no thought to this demand and they registered but it was an important step in the identification and concentration of the Jews. Another step toward the final solution was taken with the Aryanization of Jewish property.

The Kolnitchanski family was unaware of the steps being taken to deprive them of their ability to earn a living. From the National Archives of Paris,[237] I acquired a thick file of documents that clearly describe how the Kolnitchanski pocketbook business was Aryanized. At the very core of the process was the appointment of Provisional Administrators, non-Jews who took control of, and attempted to profit from, the business. The anti-Semitism of the two administrators appears in some of the documents. One document stands out in shedding light on what happened to the property of the Kolnitchanski's.

The first document (Recepisse) is a request for a renewal of a license.
Recepisse
1. Request for renewal of license
2. D'inscription Modificative
Mr. Bourrel informs the Department of Commerce, concerned with the registration of documents, that he will take over the business.
My grandmother's number was 464466 (du registre analytique)
Notarized: cadre reserve a la legalesation de la signature
3. Bureaux transference. Date taken over: 3/12/41

Actifs des bicans (pas de comptabilite: no trace of bookkeeping)
Chiffres (sales) 1938 to today
Montant: none (the most she ever made)

Business owners needed a license and a number in order to sell their merchandise. With document No. 27458 D'inscription Modificative, the Aryanization process was underway. With this form, the appointed provisional administrator, Mr. Bourrel (his address and date of birth appear on the document) took over my grandmother's pocketbook selling business. Also in the document, the transfer bureau formally noted the date of the takeover as 3/12/41. The confirmation of transfer went through the Prefecture de Police. Since her license and her number had been declared invalid, Dora Kolnitchanski could no longer legally work as a pocketbook seller. She had her business stolen from her as of March 12, 1941. As of early 1942, ". . .4,540 of 26,570 such enterprises"[238] were Aryanized. The legality of the document is supported by its notorization, a reference to "cadre reserve a la legalisation de la signature."

Notaries played a significant role in Aryanization. ". . .after the law of 22 July 1941, all transfers of covered Jewish property held by A.P.'s had to

Costs involved in the takeover of Dora Kolnitchanski's pocketbook business

R. BOURREL
Commissaire-Gérant
7, Bld. Haussmann
P A R I S (9ª)

Tél. Prov. 79-30

Bureaux transférés : 9 Bld. des Chaoaines
                              Tel. Cadet 75-07

Paris,le 7 Janvier 194_

RAPPORT ENTREPRISE ISRAELITE- CARREAU DU TEMPLE

- Sans boutique -

Nº du DOSSIER 370
Section I.C.

NOM: Mme KOLNITCHANSKI   PRENOM : Divorjra Lita

Adresse : 140. rue de Ménilmontant à Paris

Nationalité : Française par mariage en 1920

Objet du Commerce : Brocanteur (Carreau du Temple)

Registre de Commerce : radiation faite (jointe)

Carte d'acheteur : rendue au Comité du Textile N'en possédait pas
Médaille : rendue au Carreau du Temple

Patente : radiation faite

Marchandises : Stock vendu (voir fait si-joint)

Matériel : néant

Compte de Banque : Néant

Nº   En Banque :

Principales dettes :
          (directes - néant   Propriétaire - néant
  Impôts)
          (indirectes - néant   Fournisseurs - néant

Prélévements effectués :   Estimation :

    1ª - Frais gestion........   1ª - Frais gestion.........

    2ª - Honoraires ....   2ª - Honoraires ....

MISSION TERMINEE.

Je demande à être relevé de mes fonctions.

Report on my grandmother's "Jewish business"

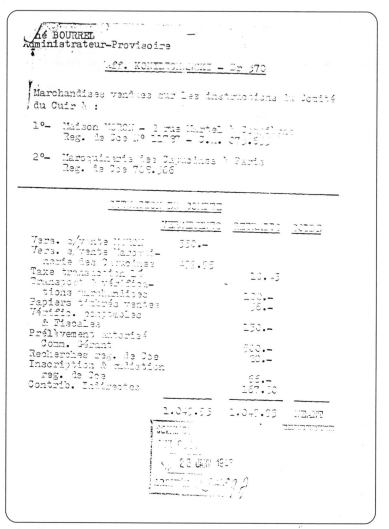

Value placed on Dora Kolnitchanski's business

COMMISSARIAT GÉNÉRAL
AUX
QUESTIONS JUIVES

N° ....

SERVICE DU CONTROLE
des
ADMINISTRATEURS PROVISOIRES

NOMINATION

Vu l'Ordonnance allemande en date du 18 octobre 1940,

Vu l'Ordonnance allemande en date du 26 avril 1941,

relatives aux mesures contre les Juifs

Vu la Note Wi I Az 7103/41 en date du 7 mai 1941 adressée
par le Militärbefehlshaber in Frankreich au Service du Contrôle
des Administrateurs Provisoires, relative à la nomination des
Administrateurs provisoires,

M. ....

....

....

est nommé Administrateur Provisoire de l'Entreprise :

....

....

Paris, le - 3 FEV 1943 ....

Nature de l'Entreprise : ....

....

Official date that Schuttler becomes new provisional administrator

COMMISSARIAT GENERAL AUX
QUESTIONS JUIVES

N° 3 Bis

DIRECTION GENERALE DE
L'ARYANISATION ECONOMIQUE

R.30.566 SECTION AD

Marchand ambulant

Monsieur BOURREL, 9 Bd d s Capucines PARIS
a été nommé le 12.3.41
Administrateur Provisoire de l'Entreprise KONILCKANSKY
140, rue de Ménilmontant PARIS
par la préfecture de police
sur la proposition de
cet Administrateur Provisoire a été relevé de ses fonctions
Motif du relèvement faute grave de gestion

J'ai nommé Administrateur Provisoire Monsieur SCHUTTLER 81
Bd Richard Lenoir PARIS par ordre de nomination Nr R. 30.566

NOTA - La Section certifie qu'aucune correspondance n'a été échangée
avec les Autorités d'Occupation au sujet de ce remplacement.

Schuttler replaces Bourrel as provisional administrator of Dora Kolnitchanski's business

COMMISSARIAT GENERAL AUX
QUESTIONS JUIVES

N°376 P.

DIRECTION GENERALE DE
L'ARYANISATION ECONOMIQUE

MODELE A

DECISION

relative au paiement de frais d'administration provisoire
et de contrôle d'une entreprise déficitaire ou dont les disponibilités
ne permettent pas de supporter ces charges

Monsieur *Schuttler* demeurant à *Paris - 81 av. Richard Lenoir*
(compte en banque n° 460 84 - 6 dit *Lyonnais - J 45 B. Voltaire*
a été nommé Administrateur Provisoire de l' Entreprise *Konilchansky*
140 rue Ménilmontant

du 12. 2. 43 au

En application des dispositions de l'arrêté irterministériel
du 6 octobre 1941, sa rémunération a été fixée
mensuellement (
forfaitairement (1 à 900
pour mois (1)
et arrêté à un total de *deux cents frs*

17 MAI 1944

Monies to be paid for Schuttler's takeover of my grandmother's business

```
      JF JL
SECTION : I.C        ETABLISSEMENT DE LA REMUNERATION            N°606 P.

                  (de                                                  DOSSIER
AFFAIRE : (1)     (entre                                               N° 17.435
                  (au-dessous de          50.000  "

NOM et ADRESSE de l'AFFAIRE .
NOM et ADRESSE de l'A.P.
Nommé le   Février  1947 O.M. n°         (1) par
Prise effective de fonctions le  6/  /1947    - Cessation le
---------------------------------------------------------------------------
    CHIFFRES D'AFFAIRES       : REMUNERATION :     Le PRELEVEMENT
    Exercices de DOUZE mois.  : Théorique    :  doit être fait sur :
(L'A.P. doit fournir les bilans ou : d'après le :
une déclaration du Bureau du Chif-:   barème   :
fre d'Affaires) (feuille jaune    :           :
                                  :           :
 - 1938 :                         :           :            COMPTE 511
                                  :           :
 - 1939 :                         :           :  (1)
                                  :           :
 - 1940 :                         :           :
                                  :           :      OBSERVATIONS :
 - 1941 :                         :           :
                                  :           :
 - 1942 :
---------------------------------------------------------------------------
1°/ Appréciation sur le travail de l'A.P. 2°/ Indiquer s'il y a un mandataire
    Liquidateur judiciaire ou Syndic de faillite (date) 3°/ Entreprise ouver-
    te - fermée 4°/ Indiquer les circonstances spéciales, lorsque le barème
    ne peut s'appliquer.



Versement à la Treuhand (1)                              - Pas lieu à versement
---------------------------------------------------------------------------
PROPOSITION du CHEF de SECTION :




(1) - Rayer les mentions inutiles.
```

How payment is made and negotiated with provisional administrators

```
            II est autorisé par le présent à recevoir une somme de  200.
            (à l'acompte
à titre     (de solde d'une mensualité
(I)         (de mandatement pour solde de la totalité de la rémunération
             accordée

            L'entreprise n'étant pas en état de supporter cette charge la
somme de          200,           ci-dessus mentionnée sera en application
de l'article 22 de la loi du 22 Juillet 1941, réglée à M. x  Schuttler
par M. le Payeur Général de la Seine sur le compte  ouvert dans ses écritu-
res au nom du Commissaire Général aux Questions juives et contre remise
de la présente décision acquittée par l'Administrateur Provisoire (pour
les paiements inférieurs à 3.000 Frs; les sommes supérieures devant être
virées à un compte bancaire au nom de l'Administrateur Provisoire).

                              Paris, le

                 Le Directeur Général  de l'Aryanisation
                            Economique :




(I) -Rayer les mentions inutiles
```

Compensation to Schuttler for management of Dora Kolnitchanski's business

be approved by the CGQJ, and in the Occupation Zone by the Germans, too. Notaries must be so informed, writes CGQJ in early September..."[239]

The so-called legal justification for the Aryanization of my grandmother's business appears in document R.30.737, the German ordinances of October 18, 1940 and April 26, 1941. These ordinances had been preceded by the earlier one of September 27, 1940, which settled the issues of who was a Jew and how to concentrate Jews in the occupied zone. The seizure of Jewish business large and small in according with the October 18th ordinance meant that ". . .all Jewish enterprises in the Occupied Zone were to be registered and placed under trusteeship — not merely those that had been abandoned by owners in flight." [240]

In the lefthand corner of the document, the reference is to SCAP, which chose the French trustees, known as Administrateurs Provisoires. The ultimate legal authority responsible for the Administrateurs Provisoires, was the MBF or Militarbefehlshaber, the German military High Command. The theft of Jewish property extended to any profits made from the sale of the property by the April 26th ordinance. It included another provision which forbade them to exercise numerous careers.

On this document dated January 7, 1943, the name of the Provisional Administrator and address appears in the lefthand corner. On the bottom of the page, with the date stamped January 23, 1943, is the Commissariat General Aux Questions Juives. "The work of Aryanization...

IV/SL SECTION I.C
Affaire: KOLNITCHANSKY
Dossier: 17.000/2??

e ??. ???

Monsieur;

Comme suite à votre rapport concernant
cette entreprise, j'ai l'honneur de vous in-
former que les ?????? ?? manquent dans cette affaire sont les radiations au Registre
du Commerce et au Rôle de la Patente.

Je vous signale que je fais ce jour une
demande d'enquête pour ????? et d'avoir l'a-
dresse du juif.Dès que j'aurai obtenu une
réponse,je vous tiendrai au courant.

Veuillez agréer, Monsieur,l'assurance de
mes sentiments distingués.

Monsieur SCHUTTLER
81,Bd Richard Lenoir
-PARIS-.

Schuttler's request for the "address of the Jew" (Dora Kolnitchanski)

came to absorb two thirds of the Commissariat's activity. . ."[241] On the
left hand side, next to this section is I.C., a reference to the section that
concerns itself with the management of certain business. Also relevant in
this document under the heading Prelevements effectues, there are expenses for the business (titre de frais de gestion) and salary (a titre
d'honoraires). The sum for each was 500 francs.

There is no doubt whatsoever as to the nature of the next document
Rapport Enterprise Israelite dated January 7, 1943, which had a reference to the Carreaux du Temple where Dora Kolnitchanski sold pocketbooks without a store (sans boutique). Her carte d'Acheteur or license to
sell, (a part of the Aryanization process) was turned over to the Carreaux
du Temple. On the bottom of this document, the Provisional Adminis-

Bourrel is thanked for giving the correct "name of the Jew"

trator, Mr. Bourrel, indicates that he wants out, possibly to get into another business.

Once taken over, the AP had the freedom to do as he pleased with the business. The documents are clear evidence of the power APs had to use and transfer a business. Mr. Bourrel was following the common procedure to transfer the business to another Aryan owner.

What followed the preceding document was a breakdown of items — pocketbooks sold — at the Carreaux du Temple. Numbers one and two indicate to whom they were sold and various costs, such as bills of

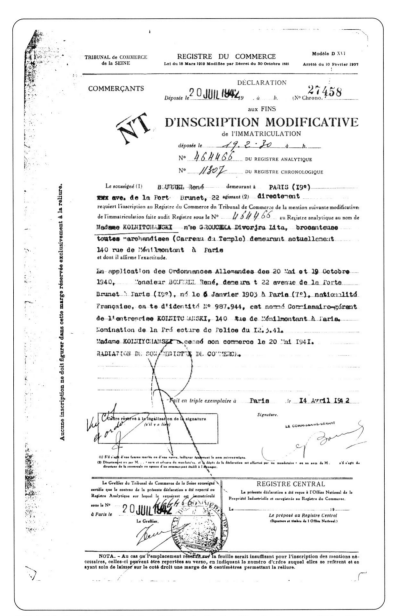

TRIBUNAL de COMMERCE
de la SEINE

REGISTRE DU COMMERCE
Loi du 18 Mars 1919 Modifiée par Décret du 30 Octobre 1935

Modèle D XVI
Arrêté du 10 Février 1937

COMMERÇANTS

DÉCLARATION

Déposée le 20 JUIL 1942 19 . à h. (N° Chrono. 27458

aux FINS

D'INSCRIPTION MODIFICATIVE
de l'IMMATRICULATION

déposée le _19.2.30_ à h.

N° _464466_ DU REGISTRE ANALYTIQUE

N° _11307_ DU REGISTRE CHRONOLOGIQUE

Le soussigné (1)   BOURREL René   demeurant à   PARIS (19°)
XXX ave. de la Port Brunet, 22 agissant (2)   directement
requiert l'inscription au Registre du Commerce du Tribunal de Commerce de la mention suivante modificative:
de l'immatriculation faite audit Registre sous le N° _464466_ au Registre analytique au nom de
Madame KOLNITCHANSKI   née GROUCHKA Divorjra Lita,   brocanteuse
toutes marchandises (Carreau du Temple) demeurant actuellement
140 rue de Ménilmontant à Paris
et dont il affirme l'exactitude.

En application des Ordonnances Allemandes des 20 Mai et 19 Octobre
1940, Monsieur BOURREL René, demeurant 22 avenue de la Porte
Brunet à Paris (19°), né le 6 Janvier 1903 à Paris (7°), nationalité
Française, carte d'identité N° 987.944, est nommé Commissaire-gérant
de l'entreprise KOLNITCHANSKI, 140 Rue de Ménilmontant à Paris.
Nomination de la Préfecture de Police du 12.3.41.
Madame KOLNITCHANSKI a cessé son commerce le 20 Mai 1941.
RADIATION DE SON REGISTRE DE COMMERCE.

Fait en triple exemplaire à   Paris   le   14 Avril 1942

Cadre réservé à la légalisation de la signature
(s'il y a lieu)

Signature.

LE COMMISSAIRE-GÉRANT

(1) S'il s'agit d'une femme mariée ou d'une veuve, indiquer également le nom patronymique.
(2) Directement ou par M. . . . son et adresse du mandataire, si le dépôt de la déclaration est effectué par un mandataire - ou au nom de M. . . s'il s'agit du directeur de la commercial en agence d'un commerçant établi à l'étranger.

Le Greffier du Tribunal de Commerce de la Seine soussigné
certifie que le contenu de la présente déclaration a été reporté au
Registre Analytique sur lequel le requérant est immatriculé
sous le N° _464466_
à Paris le   20 JUIL 1942
Le Greffier.

REGISTRE CENTRAL

La présente déclaration a été reçue à l'Office National de la
Propriété Industrielle et enregistrée au Registre du Commerce.
Le _____ 19__.
Le préposé au Registre Central
(Signature et timbre de l'Office National.)

NOTA. - Au cas où l'emplacement réservé sur la feuille serait insuffisant pour l'inscription des mentions nécessaires, celles-ci peuvent être reportées au verso, en indiquant le numéro d'ordre auquel elles se réfèrent et en ayant soin de laisser sur le coté droit une marge de 5 centimètres permettant la reliure.

Aucune inscription ne doit figurer dans cette marge réservée exclusivement à la reliure.

Official theft of Dora Kolnitchanski's pocketbook-selling business as of May 20, 1941

sales. That document is proof that the AP believed the business was not the profit-maker he had hoped for. The sale of my grandmother's merchandise also meant it was a business, like so many other businesses, that "added nothing to the French economy, they were to be liquidated and the assets auctioned off." [242]

In a document dated February 3, 1943, the name Schuttler appears as a replacement for Mr. Bourrel. For numbers R. 30.666 and R. 30.566 and R. 30.737 there appears specific relevant information. Schuttler draws a salary of 500 F. The reason for his nomination was due to faute grave de gestion or mismanagement, incompetence on the part of Mr. Bourrel. It was the Service de Controle des Administrateurs Provisoires or SCAP which had the final say as to who became an A.P. Input as to the individuals chosen may have come from Comites d'organisation. "From the beginning, the Ministry of Industrial Production consulted these associates about whom to name as Administrateurs Provisoires."[243]

What is significant in the document Etablissement de la Remuneration or request for payment provides an explanation of how payment is made and negotiated with the Provisional Administrators. In effect, since Dora Kolnitchanski's business could not afford to pay his salary, he will be paid by the bureau in charge of Aryanization, a salary of 200 F. The reason, as explained in the document, is that if the salary is under 3000 F., the bureau pays it. A salary over 3000 F via direct deposit goes into a bank.

For some reason, from the documents dated February 16, 1943, there was some confusion over the spelling and correct location of the appropriated business. Schuttler wrote a number of requests to determine the exact spelling of the name and location of the business.

In a number of correspondences, the virulent anti-Semitism is a striking feature in these documents. For example, there is a November 4, 1943 document in which Schuttler demands to know "l'addresse du Juif." In Schuttler's November 25, 1943 letter, he said, "Will you give the surname and address of that Jew, so I can pursue my mission." In the final letter, dated April 17, 1943, answered by Bourrel, the issue of the correct spelling is cleared up. Bourrel is thanked for his precise communication "of the exact spelling of the Jew." In a strange twist of fate, it was during June 1941, around the time Dora Kolnitchanski lost her pocketbook business that my grandfather (Motke or Max) was opening with a partner his own butcher store in the Bronx.

Not all family members were only content to carry on with life as before. This was the case with my Uncle Albert. I consider myself very fortunate to have known him from his visits with us in the U.S. and my

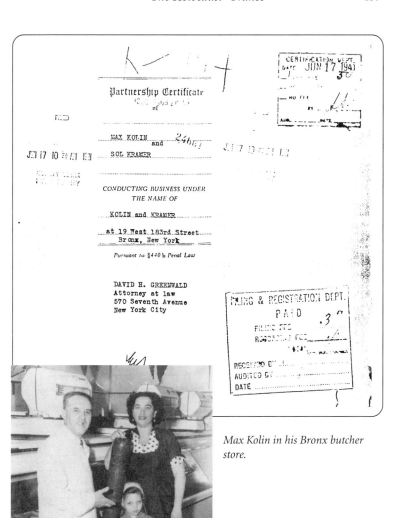

Max Kolin in his Bronx butcher
store.

Certificate of Partnership

The undersigned do hereby certify that they *(intend to) (now) conduct or transact business under a partnership agreement under the name and style of

KOLIN and KRAMER

at   19 West 183rd Street
in the County of   Bronx   , State of New York, and do further certify that the true or real full names of all the persons conducting or transacting such partnership, with the residence and business addresses of such persons, and the age of any who may be infants, are as follows: ,

†NAME	RESIDENCE	BUSINESS ADDRESS
MAX KOLIN	1347 Prospect Avenue. Bronx, New York	19 West 183rd Street. Bronx, New York
SOL KRAMER	1695 Hoe Avenue Bronx, New York	19 West 183rd Street. Bronx, New York

In Witness Whereof, We have this 16th day of   June   1941 , made and signed this certificate.

Max Kolin

Sol Kramer

State of New York
County of BRONX   } ss.:

On this   16th   day of   June   , 19 41 , before me personally appeared

MAX KOLIN and SOL KRAMER

to me known and known to me to be the individuals described in, and who executed the foregoing certificate, and they   thereupon   duly acknowledged to me that they   executed the same.

*Cross out words not used.
†Specify which are infants and state ages.

visits to Paris in the 1960's, 1970's and 1980's. Unfortunately, the idea of writing a book came later on, and he passed away before I was able to question him about his role in the French Resistance. What is known about his role comes from my mother and aunt.

If there is a single impression I have of my Uncle Albert, it is of some-one with strongly held ideas and convictions. This explains why he was so active in the French Resistance. His resistance took on many forms. In the 20e, he was active with his best friend, Ferdinand Zalkinof. Their resistance work was through the F.T.P., a Communist-led group with many Jewish members.

Jews were in the forefront of resistance against the German occupa-tion forces. "Immigrant Jewish Communists led the urban guerrilla cam-paign against the Nazis and collaborators. Proportionately, they suffered the heaviest casualties of any French fighting unit." [244] The Jews were well-represented in fighting the Nazis: ". . .25 percent of the Jewish commu-nity was involved in resistance work." [245]

Zalkinof was one of the participants in an early act of resistance in the metro Barbes. He also had a role in another act of resistance in the 17e. "Le 10 et 11 Septembre, une attaque massive avec des bouteilles d'essence et des cocktails Molotov eut lieu contre un garage de l'armee Allemade, situe au 21, boulevard Pershing, dans le 17e arrondissement. Deux groupes intervinrent, composes de Lucien (Miret Must), Marcel Boundaries, Gilbert Brustlein, Ferninand Zalkinof. . ." [246]

In a supreme act of sacrifice, Zalkinof and other members of his organization allowed themselves to be caught "so their leader could es-cape the clutches of the German Police." [247] He and other resistance mem-bers were put on trial on March 4, 1942, for two days. They were charged with the following crimes on March 5:

> The accused, all French nationals, are seven in number, including one Jew and one-half Jew. All belong to the Communist party. They have perpetrated every kind of attack on the German Army, and it has been established from the accusation files that, in the actions of which they were guilty, they were inspired not by pa-triotic motives, but by the slavish obedience to article 25 of the Communist party program drawn up at the Sixth Congress in Moscow in 1928. . .These are not, therefore, ordinary terrorists, but assailants belonging to a group which was fully organized even before the German occupation and authorized to commit mis-deeds and crimes under any government, provided it was in ac-cordance with the dictates of the Kremlin. [248]

Zalkinof was eventually caught and executed in March 1942. He was eighteen years old. Just prior to his execution, he wrote and sent this poignant letter to his parents:

E - Qui étaient-ils?

Il serait nécessaire de remettre en lumière ces femmes, ces hommes, ces résistants.
Ceux que le nazisme a effacé de nos vies, ces jeunes filles et garçons dont l'avenir s'est arrêté devant un peloton d'exécution ou dans un camp.
Ceux qui ont poursuivi, poursuivent leur combat pour la liberté et la paix.
Quelques uns doivent à leurs amis de nous laisser leur message de vie et d'espoir.

Lettres de résistants fusillés.

Fernand ZALKINOV

Jeune militant du XXe arrondissement.
Boursier, étudiant de l'Ecole Arago.
Engagé dans les F.T.P.,
arrêté et exécuté par les Allemands
à l'âge de 18 ans

Paris, le 9 mars 1942

Mon cher papa, ma chère maman,

Ceci est ma dernière lettre. Dans quelques heures, je serai mort. Je suis très courageux et très calme. Ne pleurez pas, je vous en prie, mais pensez à moi. Il faut que vous soyez forts, comme je le suis. Dites-vous bien que je suis mort d'une belle mort et que, plus tard, vous serez fiers de moi.
Je vous ai profondément aimés et je sais combien vous me chérissez.
J'ai vécu si heureux, grâce à vous, à tout ce que vous avez fait pour moi.
Je vous l'ai bien mal rendu, mais je sais que vous ne m'en voulez pas.
Je préfère ne pas vous avoir vus. Je n'ai pas cessé de penser à vous. Et vous, pensez à moi,et c'est pourquoi je suis si courageux.
Je vous demande pardon de tout ce que vous avez souffert par ma faute; je sais que vous me pardonnerez parce que vous m'avez tant aimé et que vous oublierez tout le mal que je vous ai fait.
Je suis très calme et j'attends dans une parfaite tranquillité d'âme. J'ai conscience que ma mort n'aura pas été inutile. Il ne faut pas que vous pleuriez. Soyez forts comme je le suis. Songez que plus tard vous serez fiers de moi et vous en aurez le droit. Jurez-moi que vous serez courageux et je mourrai tranquille.
N'oubliez pas que vous avez encore d'autres enfants et j'espère que plus tard vous aurez aussi des petits-enfants dans lesquels vous pourrez me revoir et me reconnaître.

Aujourd'hui, je rêve à ce que furent mes années d'enfance et je suis si heureux en me rappelant votre amour. Croyez bien que je vous ai toujours *aimés et que si je vous ai fait souffrir, je ne le voulais pas. Mais il le fallait. Il fallait que je fasse mon devoir, quoiqu'il m'en coûte. Encore une fois, je vous demande pardon.*
Ne laissez pas salir ma mémoire. Dites-vous bien que j'ai fait tout ce que j'ai pu pour rester propre et honnête, pour être digne de vous.
J'aurai vécu et je serai mort pour quelque chose, pour la cause que j'ai toujours servie avec le plus grand amour et je ne regrette pas mon sacrifice, car je sais qu'il ne sera pas vain.
Je suis courageux parce que c'est la mort que j'aurais choisie. Je ne veux pas que vous pleuriez, cela me ferait trop de peine. Pensez beaucoup à moi et cela me rendra plus fort.
Je suis sûr que plus tard il y aura un monde de joie et d'amour.
Alors vous penserez à moi.
Adieu. Adieu pour toujours, mon cher papa, ma chère petite maman. Je vous embrasse de toute mon âme de fils aimant et je vous presse sur mon coeur pour qu'une dernière fois vous me donniez votre chaleur et que vous m'en enveloppiez. Cela fait tellement de bien.
Je vous aime et je vous embrasse. Adieu.

Fernand

Fernand Zalkinow (1923 - 1942)
Portrait dessiné, appartenant à
Mme Juliette Fisz née Goutverg.

AVIS

1. **HANLET**, Roger, de Paris.
2. **SEMAHYA**, Acher, de Paris.
3. **PELTIER**, Robert, de Gous-
sainville.
4. **RIZO**, Christian, de Paris.
5. **BLONCOURT**, Louis, de Paris,
6. **MILAN**, Pierre, de Paris.
7. **ZALKINOW**, Fernand, de
Paris.

ont été condamnés à mort
comme francs-tireurs et pour
s'être livrés de concert à des
actes de violence répétés contre l'armée allemande et les
membres de celle-ci. Ils ont
été exécutés aujourd'hui.

Paris, le 9 mars 1942.
Le Commandant du Grand-Paris

FERNAND ZALKINOV
(fusillé le 9 mars 1942)

Tous les travailleurs de Belleville connaissaient bien la famille Zalkinov,
la famille du cordonnier... Il n'avait que des amis dans les organisations
juives progressistes et parmi les diffuseurs du journal « La Presse Nouvelle ». Et c'est à ses amis qu'il devait dire un jour : « J'ai trouvé ma
voie et mes enfants seront élevés dans cette voie de progrès et de
justice. »

Il trouva donc normal pendant l'Occupation que son fils, Fernand de-
vienne un courageux F.T.P. et lorsque le 9 mars 1942, il apprit, par une
lettre admirable, que celui-ci allait être fusillé pour avoir fait son devoir,
à son immense douleur se mêlait une juste fierté. Il n'hésita pas à remettre
cette lettre à ses camarades pour qu'ils la fassent circuler clandestinement
et il déclara solennellement que ses autres enfants et lui se mettaient à
la disposition de la Résistance. La Gestapo ne devait pas tarder à l'appren-
dre et elle vint arrêter le père, la mère et les enfants pour les déporter
vers les camps dont aucun ne revint.

Son père, Naoum, fut fusillé le 11 août 1942.
De cette belle famille plus rien ne subsiste, mais elle survivra à
jamais grâce à la lettre de Fernand Zalkinov que voici :

(voir ci-contre ►)

His entire family was then executed by the Nazis.

There is no doubt that the 20th Arrondissement was a hot-bed of resistance activity during the Nazi occupation. Even today, this is obvious from the large number of plaques throughout the 20th, which commemorate the people who lost their lives resisting the Nazis:

XXème ARRONDISSEMENT DE PARIS

MARS 1994

LISTE DES PLAQUES DU SOUVENIR DE LA RESISTANCE ET DE LA LIBERATION

TEXTES INTEGRAUX

3 rue Victor Dejeante

Ici habitait ETIENNE PORCHER, ouvrier boulanger, membre du PCF et de la CGT, arrêté le 24 septembre 1942. Déporté à Mathausen, le 16 avril 1943. Mort en déportation.

15 rue Belgrand

Morts pour la France

JOURIST Benjamin, fusillé par les allemands à l'âge de 27 ans. BOLLANGIER Marcel, tombé dans le maquis à l'âge de 24 ans, le 24 août 1944.

JOURDAN Maurice, tué à l'ennemi à l'âge de 20 ans, le 11 avril 1945.

5 rue Dulaure

Ici habitait Marie Thérèse FLEURY, membre du Parti Communiste Français, militante de l'Union des Femmes Françaises. Déportée comme otage, assassinée au camp d'Auschwitz le 16 avril 1943. Morte pour la France.

1 rue Dulaure

Ici habitait Hélène BRUN, membre du Parti Communiste Français, militante de l'Union des Femmes Françaises. Déportée comme otage, assassinée au camp de BERGEN-BELSEN en 1945. Morte pour la France.

63/67 Boulevard Mortier

Ici, le 24 août 1944, Henri LOUVIGNY âgé de 28 ans, est tombé à la tête de sa section F.F.I. – F.T.P.F. pour que vive la France. Reconnaissance des habitants du 20ème arrondissement.

7 avenue du Cher

> U.G.C. – U.N.F.F.I.
> Ici habitaient Mme Odile VERHULST, du réseau évasion "la
> Comette". Arrêtée le 18 janvier 1944. Déportée à
> RAVENSBRUCK. Assassinée par les nazis en février 1945.
>
> et son gendre
>
> Monsieur Vassilli LAMI, du réseau évasion "la Comette",
> arrêté le 27 juillet 1944. Déporté à NEUENGAMME.
> Assassiné par les nazis le 10 avril 1945.

84 rue des Rondeaux

> U.G.C. – U.N.F.F.I.
> Ici habitait Madame Fernande ONIMUS du réseau évasion "la
> Comette", arrêtée le 18 janvier 1944. Déportée à Ravensbruck.
> Assassinée par les nazis en Avril 1945.

226 rue des Pyrénées

> Ici habitait Maurice PILLET. Fusillé le 15 décembre 1941 à
> Châteaubriand. Mort pour la France.

6 rue d'Annam

> U.G.C. – U.N.F.F.I.
> André DULAUROY – Sous lieutenant F.F.C.I.
> Déporté à Dachau. Mort pour la France le 26 avril 1945.

155 avenue Gambetta

> Ici vécut André CHASSAGNE – F.T.P.F., mort pour que vive
> la France. Fusillé par les Allemands au Mont Valérien le 6
> octobre 1943 à l'âge de 21 ans.
> Souvenir reconnaissant des habitants.

13 rue St Blaise

> Ici vivait Cadix SOSNOWSKI. F.T.P Français. Fusillé par les Allemands à l'âge de 17 ans. Mort pour la France le 26 mai 1943.

13 rue St Blaise

> Ici habitait BROBION Henri. F.T.P.F. Soldat de la brigade Fabien. Tombé au champ d'honneur le 18 janvier 1945 à HABSHEIM Alsace.

55 Rue Planchat

> Dans cet immeuble, habitait Louis Georges PICOT. Membre du parti communiste français. Assassiné par les nazis au camp d'AUSCHWITZ le 19 septembre 1942.

66 rue des Orteaux (poste de police)

> A la mémoire du gardien de la paix, Georges AMODRU. Arrêté par les Allemands le 18 août 1941. Mort en déportation le 7 mai 1945 au camp de TSROSBERG

Avenue Gambetta (Commissariat central – Mairie du XXè)

> A la mémoire du brigadier Louis FLEURY, mort pour la France à la libération de Paris le 26 août 1944.

7 place Gambetta

> Ici habitait Jacques KRAMKIMEL, 21 ans, capitaine F.T.P.F. 35 ème brigade. Mort pour la France dans la lutte contre l'occupant nazi.

7 place Gambetta

> Ici habitait Léon JOSSELOVITZ, 40 ans, commandant F.T.P.F. Mort pour la France dans la lutte contre l'occupant nazi. Membre du parti communiste français.

Rue de Ménilmontant (pont du chemin de fer)

> A la mémoire des héros tombés le 23 août 1944 à l'attaque victorieuse des trains nazis.
> BOLTZ François 38 ans, GODEFROY Louis 53 ans, ADJEMAN 50 ans et deux patriotes inconnus. Gloire immortelle – Morts pour la France.

23 rue d'Eupatoria

> Au numéro 15 de ce passage habitait André DURAND, adjudant F.T.P.F, arrêté par la police de Vichy et fusillé par les hitlériens le 24 mars 1944 à l'âge de 21 ans.
> Souvenir reconnaissant des habitants.

18 rue de Tourtille

> Ici demeurait NADEL Simon, membre de la LICA. Fusillé par les Allemands comme otage le 15 décembre 1941 à l'âge de 45 ans.

46 rue Ramponneau (poste de police)

> A notre collègue André PERRIN, mort pour la France et la libération de Paris le 19 août 1944.

48 rue Ramponneau

> Ici demeurait Albert CHELBLUNS, membre de la LICA. Maquisard. Mort pour la France le 14 janvier 1945 à l'âge de 20 ans.

9/11 rue des Envierges

> Ici habitait GODEFROY Louis, mort pour la libération de Paris le 23 août 1944.
> Libération Nord – 20ème section   Groupe Piat.

36 Boulevard de Charonne

Ici sont tombés pour la libération de Paris, le 22 Août 1941,
trois F.F.I. : DUPUIS Maurice 22 ans, BALDACHINO Richard
42 ans, DACHER Jean 22 ans. Honneur à leur mémoire.

PLAQUES DU SOUVENIR DANS LES ENTREPRISES

| ALLENO | Dépôt RATP 18 rue des Pyrénées |

| FORTHOFFER | Dépôt RATP, rue de Lagny |

| BILLOT René | Métro Pelleport |

| Marie Thérèse FLEURY | Bureau Central PTT rue des Pyrénées. |

My Uncle David Kolnitchanski, whom I was fortunate to have met
frequently in Paris also was active in the French Resistance, through his
affiliation with the Communists. Before and after his war, he made his
living as a pocketbook maker. He was always very well-dressed, with a
beret, and coat and tie, no matter what the occasion. He always carried a
book with him.

In many ways, Albert was like David in that both of them held strong
political views and took action. David was a die-hard Communist, and
every Sunday, he stood on a Paris street corner and sold L'Humanite, the
party newspaper. Unfortunately, David passed away on August 6,1985,
many years before this research began. The obituary in Le Monde speaks
volumes about his role in the French Resistance, noting that he was
awarded the Medaille de la resistance, the Croix de guerre, 1939-1945
and the Maquis de L'Aveyron (F.T.P.).

Albert continued his resistance work until a fellow traveler was arrested and tortured. He denounced him. Upon learning of this fact, Albert
fled to Avignon, a logical choice at the time, since at the time, it was in
the free zone. Nonetheless, the Germans sent an arrest warrant out for
the name Kolnitchanski. My grandfather, Robert, was also at this time in

Adolph Weisser in Paris, date unknown

Avignon, working and trying to locate an apartment for the family to join him.

My mother recalls that everyday at 7 a.m. French police in plainclothes came to the apartment to look for a man named Kolnitchanski. My grandmother protested this intrusion and lied to the police, stating that my grandfather was a low-life who had deserted two children and a wife. The Germans sent to the French police in the unoccupied zone an arrest warrant for Kolnitchanski. My grandfather was arrested because he had the same last name.

Albert knew the police were looking for him and he let himself be arrested so that my grandfather could be released. The thing that hurt him the most was that he had to cross the town, wearing handcuffs like a common criminal.

It did not take long for news to reach the family of Albert's arrest. Adolph was well-aware that his mother and sisters were in need of support. In no uncertain terms, Adolph told them, "You are three women, you should not be left alone." This remark was his putting into practice the meaning of his name as "noble helper." The day after he spoke those words, he was arrested in a raid. My mother remembers that it was the December 12, 1941 roundup of Jews in Paris.

The raid was intended to capture notable Jews from professional backgrounds. Planning and capture of them was carefully planned. This fact means that in all likelihood Adolph was arrested as one of 54 Jews caught during the l'heure de dejeuner in a roundup "dans les grands restaurants". [249]

Specific groups were targetted by this roundup, including Jewish professionals, intellectuals, and decorated war veterans, considered the most distinguished members of the Jewish community, and all of them French citizens. Most were arrested in their homes. In addition, a number of foreign Jews were arrested at random on the streets of Paris. It can be stated with some certainty that Max was one of these. In fact, according to the French government, he was considered a stateless Jew. [250]

From December 12, 1941 until March 27, 1942, he was in the Jewish camp of Compieigne, established to accomodate prisoners of the December roundup. The Jewish Camp, given the Letter C was one of the three camps, the two others B housed those arrested as communists and camp A for Russian prisoners of war. The three camps were separated by double rows of barbed wire. Within Camp C, prisoners were housed in either block 5 for French Jews or 7 for foreign-born Jews. The Jews confined were classified into one of three categories, according to Dannecker's Feb. 10, 1942 letter sent to the military high command: those intended for deportation, those identified as hostages for reprisals and those identified as Jews.

Conditions for Jewish prisoners were harsh and crude. Housed in barracks until the end of January, the prisoners slept on straw on an ice-cold cement floor, then they were provided with mattresses. There was no furniture, such as tables or chairs. With no heating, it was almost as cold inside as outside. Absent from the camp was a hospital and the camp was not permitted to receive medication from the outside.

I wonder how Adolph coped with these conditions. What went through his mind at this time, since with the exception of a limited number of duties, he would pass the time with nothing to do. He had plenty of time to think about what his captors had in store for him and the other prisoners. I suspect he had another thought that preoccupied him, that is, concern for the rest of the family, in particular, his little sisters and his mother, especially in the absence of his brother and father.

From the time of his arrest until March 12, Adolph was prohibited from having any communication with family members. Prisoners in Camps A and B were permitted to write to relatives and request care packages, but not those in the Jewish camp. In a January 15, 1942 letter, the Red Cross requested that Jews be permitted to correspond with relatives. In spite of Dannecker's official denial of this request, behind the scenes, camp officers as of January 28 and in the end of February, established an imposed form letter that the prisoners should follow when writing to relatives.

Adolph's letter to the family, sent a few weeks before he was deported, conforms to the strict guidelines, a sample of which is included here, in terms of what can be discussed and items requested for use.

"Mon cher, je me porte bien. J'ai droit a trois colis pas mois de cinq kilos chacun, contentenant nourriture, linge, vetements, chausseurs, objets de toilettes, tabac...Vous pouvez m'envoyer, sans limite de poids, un colis ou valise de linge, chausseurs, vetements et objets de toilette." [251]

In fact, the exact date when prisoners could write and request various items was March 12; "two weeks later, steps were taken to deport the prisoners to Auschwitz on March 26." [252] About 640 people were led into the courtyard. Their names were read out loud and separated from the remaining 80 men were those married to Aryan women, one of many categories of prisoners in Compeigne.

They were interned for three months before they were given permission to write. The letter was the last time the family heard from Adolph. On the front of the envelope there is the stamped "Frontstalag 122," which was "the name given to Compeigne as of June 9, 1940 to house French

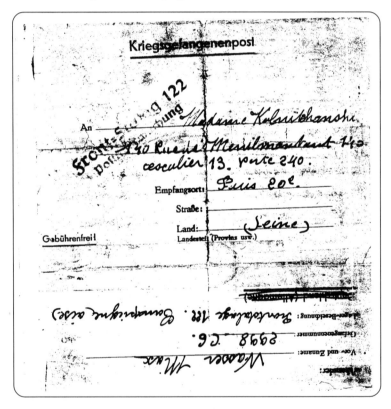

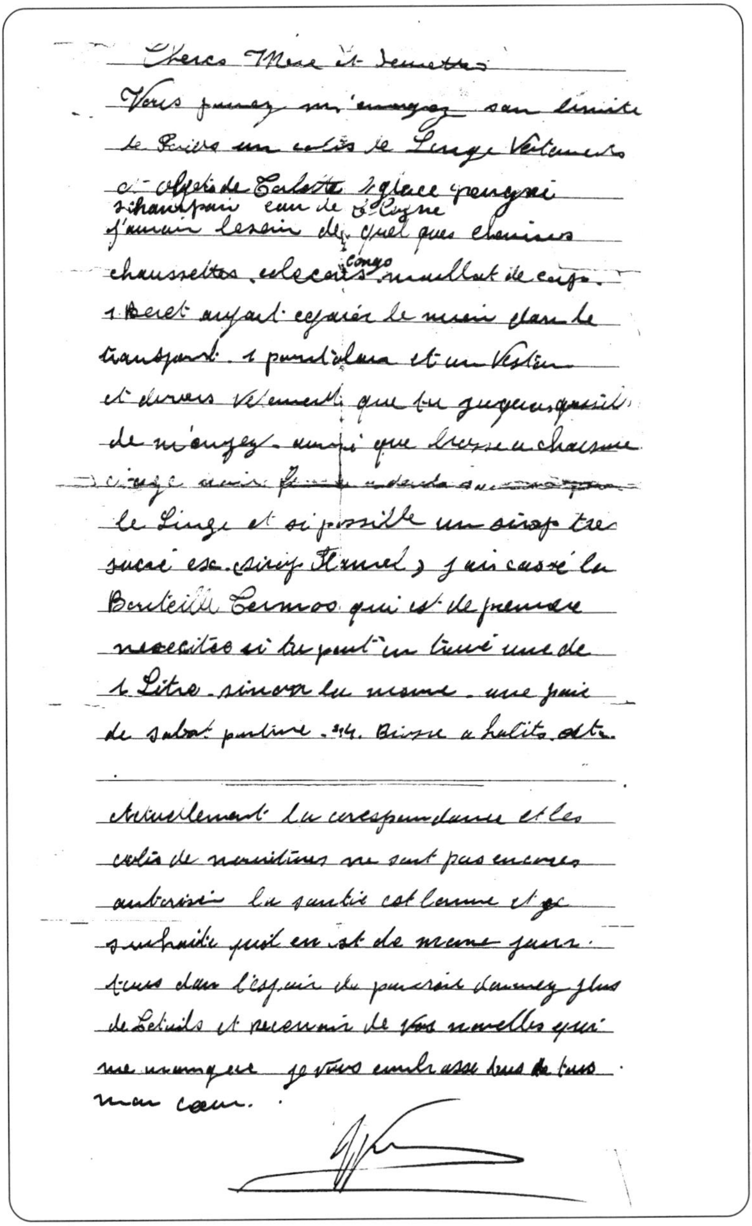
Chers Mère et Demettes
Vous pouvez m'envoyez sans limite
de Poids un colis de Linge Vêtements
et Objets de Toilette 1 glace peigne
shampoin eau de Cologne
j'aurais besoin de quel ques chemises
chaussettes caleçons congo maillot de corps.
1 Beret ayant egaré le mien dans le
transport. 1 pantalon et un Veston
et divers vêtements que tu jugeras qu'il
de m'envoyez ainsi que brosse a chaussure
[illegible]
le Linge et si possible un sirop tres
sucré ex. sirop [illegible] j'ai cassé la
Bouteille Termos qui est de premiere
necessités si tu peut en trouvé une de
1 Litre sinon la meme. une paire
de sabot pointure 34. Brosse a habits. etc.

Actuellement la correspondance et les
colis de nourritures ne sont pas encores
autorisé la santé est bonne et je
souhaite qu'il en est de meme pour
tous dans l'espoir de pouvoir donnez plus
de details et recevoir de vos nouvelles qui
me manquent je vous embrasse tous de tout
mon cœur.

Adolph's letter

and British prisoners of war, and later, political prisoners." [253]
> Dear Mother and little sisters:
> You can send me without weight limitations a package of linen,
> clothing, toiletries, one mirror, one comb, shampoo, cologne wa-
> ter. I will also be in need of a few shirts, socks, underwear, T-
> shirts, a beret, because I lost mine in the transport, one pants
> and a vest and diverse clothing that you think I should have, also
> shoe brush, black shoe polish, and if possible a sweet cough syrup
> (Siroup flannel) I broke my thermos bottle which is a first neces-
> sity if you can find one of one litre, otherwise the same one as
> before, one pair of clogs and slippers.
> Actually the correspondence and the food package are not au-
> thorized for now. The health is good and I hope the same for all
> of you in the hope that I could give more detail and to receive
> news, that I miss. I kiss all of you from the bottom of my heart.

That letter was the last time the family heard from Adolph. My grandmother carried that letter with her during, and for many years after, the
war. Aunt Mina was kind enough to provide with a copy of his letter.

Adolph was one of 719 men between the ages of 21 and 54, who
made up 73% of the camp's population, in Camp C.

Material on the daily routine in Compeigne was important in providing an idea of how Adolph lived day to day. The routine never varied
from day to day. He, like everyone else, was awake at 7 a.m. and between
7 and 8 a.m. had the so-called breakfast, which consisted of colored liq-
uid that resembled coffee. Twice a day, there was roll call, in which everyone was assembled in 5 columns in front of their blocks. "Lunch was at
noon, consisting of a clear soup, which had some vegetable mixed in two
or three times a week. In addition, about 25 grams of bread and margarine was supposed to last the rest of the day." [254] Work was not mandatory
with the exception of cleaning and food preparation. The last roll call
was at four o'clock, which was followed one hour later by dinner. Around
9 p.m., lights were switched off and those who did not reach their assigned sleeping areas within 15 minutes could expect a beating.

Adolph was deported on the first convoy from France to Auschwitz
on March 27, 1942. It has been established that the exact hour of departure from Compeigne was 4 p.m. Any thought of escape was removed
when prior to their departure to the railroad station, they were surrounded
by a German detachment with fixed bayonets. To speed up the trip to the
station, many prisoners were kicked and punched. The 640 Jewish prisoners marched out of Compeigne and arrived at the railroad station,
where they were met by 550 prisoners from Drancy, all of them men

between the ages of 11 and 55, who were being deported. The justification to deport the Jews to Auschwitz arose over how best to deal with attacks on the German occupation forces. The concern of MBF commander General Otto von Stulpagel was mass executions would lead to increased resistance to the German Army. He proposed the deportation of Jews and Communists. Stulpagel resigned over this issue. The eventual solution would incorporate two approaches: executions and deportations. It was Stulpnagl's cousin, Karl Heinrich, who succeeded him and put into practice Hitler's latest command on this matter: " . . .for every subsequent outrage, not only would hostages be executed but five hundred Jews and Communists would be handed over to Himmler for deportation to the east." [255] The March 27 date was not the original date of the departure: "Deportation had been announced on 14 December. As early as January 1942, only a shortage of trains prevented the RSHA from shipping to the east a first batch of the internees held at Compiegne." [256] His name, misspelled, with the correct date of birth appears on the transport list. [257]

Much about that first convoy and the prisoners' life at Auschwitz was learned from the valuable statements given by Alter Feinsilber at the County Court of Krakow on April 13, 1945 to the Vice President of Investigations of German Nazi Crimes in Oswiecim, Edward Pechalski. He also was deported to Auschwitz on Convoy 1. His testimony is a graphic description of what Adolph's five weeks at Auschwitz were like.

> The transport consisted of 1,118 people, exclusively Jews from different countries. We were loaded into small railroad cars in groups of 50 people. As provision we each received 2.5 kg of bread and approximately 250 g of cold cuts and that was supposed to last for the duration of our transport which was supposed to last some 12 days. During the duration of the trip, we received nothing to drink. However, the transport arrived in Auschwitz within five days.
>
> When we arrived, many among us were already gone, since a number of people died because of the severe transport conditions. I want to emphasize that during the whole trip, we had received no medical assistance whatsoever.
>
> We left for Auschwitz on March 27, 1942 at 10 a.m. This was a transport consisting exclusively of adult men. When exiting, everybody wanted to take their packages which weighed approximately 25 kg per person. We had only been allowed to take packages up to that weight from France. When we arrived, the SS men who were accompanied by big dogs forbid us to take the packages with us. Nevertheless, in the rush, some of us succeeded

in taking them with us. I also want to note that when the doctors in our transport asked the SS men to at least be allowed to take the medical supplies, the SS-men replied by beating them with sticks and even shot so that several people were killed while being unloaded.

After the unloading was completed, we were lined up in rows of five and were led to the inside of the Auschwitz camp. We had to proceed at a fast rate of march, to which we were forced by beatings. Immediately after the arrival, we were directed to the bathhouse. In front of the bathhouse, we were ordered to completely undress and to put all belongings into a bag and to confirm the delivery with our own signatures. We were only allowed to take handkerchiefs into the bathhouse. In the bathhouse, we were showered with hot water which lasted for some 15 minutes. (I have to add that shortly before our departure from France, our entire bodies were shaved for which we had to pay 3 Francs.)

After the shower, we went to a different section approximately 20 to 30 meters away where we received clothes. They consisted of a shirt, underwear, wooden shoes, pants and a blouse, and a striped cap. The pans and the blouse were from Russian prisoners of war. After the clothing was accomplished, we had to do gymnastics for one hour which was conducted by one of the inmates, the elder of the barrack. The gymnastics was very tiring and the wooden boots caused wounds on the feet. During the exercise, we were not beaten but received many kicks accompanied by yelling and swearing which clearly indicated to us that we would be finished off within two days. After the exercise was over, we were led to an unfinished barrack without doors and windows, where, in the evening, we were allowed to lie down on the bare ground. Toward evening, we received our first meal in Auschwitz, which consisted of cooked turnips without bread. After dinner, we were led to block no. 11, where we were all registered which took, together with photo taking, until the morning. We found out that there was a population of some six thousand inmates in the concentration camp Auschwitz which consisted mainly of Poles, Germans as well as a few Soviet Prisoners of War. These were all men. I have not seen any women at all in camp. From this we concluded that our transport to Auschwitz was the first transport from abroad since the present inmates were partly from Poland, partly from Germany. As I already mentioned, after we were photographed, the order was passed that our whole transport had to gather, which at that moment counted approximately 1,000 men. The SS men on horses made us march at a very fast rate on a narrow path through a swamp to the camp Birkenau which was 3.5 km far away. On the way, we were, of course, beaten with batons and some were bludgeoned to death.

At the Birkenau camp itself, SS men, barrack elders and Capos were waiting for us, all with rubber or wooden batons in their hands. They all were of German nationality. They let us march through the gate inside the camp and while we were doing so, they were beating so hard on the heads with the batons, that many were bludgeoned to death at the gate. The ones after them had to jump over the bodies to get inside the camp.

After having arrived inside, we were registered and questioned about personal affairs which were not even written down. Then we were ordered to stand in the court until the roll call, which meant until 6 p.m. After the roll call, we were assigned to different barracks and I was assigned to barrack No. 13. During the roll call, we saw a group of some 60 Jews who looked terribly wasted, looked like their own shadow and were called "Muselman." Later, I found out that this name was given to inmates who were already on their last legs and looked like miserable starved fellows. Secretly, we found that they were the rest of an inmate group of 1,200 Polish Jews who had arrived two weeks before. Of this group only these few were left since all others had been murdered. After the roll call, we received coffee and bread, then we were chased into bed. For dinner, we also should have received margarine, but didn't, since, as we found out later, our superiors had simply stolen it for their own usage.

The next morning, at 3:30 a.m., we were awoken by the call bell and the morning roll call, during which we had to stand until 7 a.m. After the roll call, we received coffee and each one of us was assigned to work groups. Then we were driven out of the camp to do work until 12 p.m. From 12 to 1 p.m., was midday pause. Lunch consisted of one-half to one-quarter liter of turnip soup, although each of us should have received one liter. After lunch, it was back to work until 6 p.m. We then returned to camp, where the evening roll call took place. During this roll-call, corpses were carried out of the camp so that while the roll call lasted, the number of the block was right. After the roll call, we returned to the block for dinner where we found new corpses. We had dinner inside the block, which consisted of bread and coffee. After dinner, we were chased to bed.

That is about how every single working day looked. I have to add that during the work itself, which was extraordinarily heavy, we were beaten and thrown into the water and treated so atrociously that each day a few corpses stayed back which we then had to carry to the evening roll call. The work itself was unproductive but it was only invented to torture the inmates. We threw, for example, bricks from one place to another and carried them back to the starting point. Under such conditions, a high percentage of the inmates threw themselves into the high voltage cables; they preferred death to such living conditions. Doctor treatments did not help us at all since there were practically no drugs

One Family: Before and During the Holocaust

available. If someone went to the doctor, he was told to return to his section if he wanted to stay alive. Everyone who reported sick would be 'run-down' in the block. I add that the section elder took every opportunity to kill a human being. The higher the number of killed people, the better was his reputation. Therefore, the block elders took their advantage of the situation and slayed people who had reported in sick. I was eye-witness to a

---

LISTE DES DÉCÉDÉS À AUSCHWITZ.

CONVOI PARTI DE COMPIÈGNE-DRANCY LE 27 MARS 1942.

— 14 —

NOM ET PRÉNOMS	matricule	DATE de naissance	DATE de décès	NOM ET PRÉNOMS	matricule	DATE de naissance	DATE de décès
SCHERMAN Léo	27.732	20.12.05	9. 5.42	SYMCHOVICZ Morise	28.330	18.12.20	27. 4.42
SCHILLER Abraham	28.693	10. 3.04	17. 6.42	SZAFRAN Matys	27.787	28. 9.98	14. 8.42
SCHINFERBERG Chaim	28.015	17. 3.16	16. 5.42	SZAFRAN Frajnicz	27.786	24. 4.03	5. 5.42
SCHLATS Aron	27.809	15. 5.99	24. 4.42	SZALUTA David	27.982	18. 3.09	29. 4.42
SCHLIMMER René	28.354	11. 6.20	24. 6.42	SZAYEWICZ Chaim	27.573	8.11.02	13. 6.42
SCHMARB Marcel	27.890	19. 1.94	22. 4.42	SZLAGMAN Szlama	27.967	3. 1.13	27. 5.42
SCHOCHAT Guitel	27.861	22.10.02	15. 6.42	SZLASCHER Berke	28.197	25.12.99	1. 7.42
SCHONBERGER Maurice	28.326	7. 2.07	30. 6.42	SZMILKH S Mendel	28.584	1. 1.11	25. 6.42
SCHOTTLAND Féliks	28.082	15. 4.23	19. 6.42	SZICBPERG Mozek	28.252	19. 8.02	28. 4.42
SCHOUGRUN Andréas	28.356	3. 1.98	24. 4.42	SZPLYMGER Caroille	28.091	1. 4.12	24. 4.42
SCHOUNER Israël	28.383	26. 5.05	21. 4.42	SZWALBERG Josef	27.983	4. 3.03	23. 4.42
SCHTADZIB Moses	28.250	27. 3.96	28. 5.42	SZWARC Juda	27.848	30. 8.14	18. 6.42
SCHWAB René	27.892	22.10.07	21. 4.42	TABOUL Léo	28.580	1.10.22	29. 4.42
SCHWALBERG Marcel	28.450	4. 8.14	27. 4.42	TAUB Armand	27.949	19. 7.98	18. 4.42
SCHWARTS Léo	27.891	1. 6.99	7. 5.42	TENENBAUM David	28.310	15. 8.97	19. 4.42
SCHWEINER Gaston	27.710	8.11.19	23. 4.42	TENEBAUM Meyer	28.511	27. 4.97	7. 5.42
SEGAL Jacques	28.478	15.12.23	19. 4.42	TICKLER Hersz	28.061	10.10.03	20. 4.42
SEHNER Hermann	27.836	22. 3.22	7. 5.42	TOBOUL David	28.577	2. 9.13	26. 4.42
SIDIKADO Samy	28.371	15. 8.04	17. 6.42	TOFFEL Jankiel	27.978	20. 5.00	24. 4.42
SIEGELMAN Josef	28.156	18. 1.98	30. 4.42	TOUITOU Germain	28.578	10.11.18	27. 4.42
SILBERMAN David	28.047	28.11.11	27. 6.42	TRANSPORT Johan	27.776	18. 2.98	21. 4.42
SILBERMANN Henrich	28.611	23. 4.86	25. 4.42	TSCHERNICHOW Heiser	28.631	22.11.92	29. 4.42
SILBERMAN David	28.080	12.10.12	10. 6.42	TUVEL Jacob	28.194	15. 7.00	20. 4.42
SILMAN Israël	28.490	5. 5.02	14. 6.42	TYHOVZINSKI Jacob	27.879	26. 9.04	26. 4.42
SILMAN Jacob	28.489	13.11.94	23. 4.42	TYK Chaim	28.075	17. 8.06	2. 6.42
SIMON Samuel	27.896	20. 4.90	18. 4.42	TZIGESNITZKI Hersch	28.243	18. 8.92	29. 4.42
SIMONDS Stefan	28.022	11. 3.22	19. 4.42	ULMAN René	28.107	15. 8.01	18. 4.42
SINEZOWSKI Abraham	28.392	. 97	7. 5.42	VAN BECZESNA Raymond	28.028	4.11.19	3. 8.42
SKORNICKI David	28.499	26. 2.12	18. 5.42	VEAKSIER Isaac	28.532	20. 6.98	18. 4.42
SLADOW Benjamin	28.204	4. 4.02	10. 6.42	VEILER Jean	27.557	11. 6.02	23. 4.42
SLEDOWSKER Grégoire	27.685	18.10.07	19. 7.42	VEKERMAN Bernard	28.069	11. 2.23	29. 4.42
SLEDZ Jacques	28.526	27. 7.09	13..6.42	VELLAN Henri	27.654	4. 4.97	6. 5.42
SMILIALSKY Paul	28.148	22. 3.94	25. 4.42	VENTURA Isaac	28.547	26. 4.09	26. 5.42
SMOLIAK Raymond	27.883	12.98	25. 4.42	VIENER Aron	27.900	12. 3.99	25. 4.42
SOLNITZKI Aron	28.225	15. 1.99	7. 5.42	VOLKOVITZ Isaac	28.381	19.12.08	2. 5.42
SOKOLOWSKI Aron	28.279	15. 9.97	7. 5.42	VRONES Cham	27.822	12.12.07	17. 6.42
SONNSCHEIN Heinrich	29.300	10.12.22	20. 6.42	VUCHMAN David	28.222	8. 5.21	28. 4.42
SORBAC Roger	27.884	27. 8.91	7. 5.42	WACHSTEIN Lebja	27.548	1.10.08	17. 6.42
SOURIA Fealm	27.743	15.12.00	27. 4.42	WAJMAN Israël	28.566	12. 5.98	26. 4.42
SIPRA Moses	27.894	7. 7.14	21. 6.42	WAJNCYGIER Zélie	28.538	4.10.98	29. 5.42
SPIWAK Geozin	28.352	27. 7.98	28. 4.42	WAJNNAM Vajach	27.549	20.12.06	21. 4.42
STARK Heinrich	28.054	9. 9.99	3. 5.42	WAJSBAND Boris	28.445	9. 8.98	7. 5.42
STEFANSKI Heinrich	28.108	13. 4.06	3. 5.42	WALCSMANN David	28.017	26. 7.95	24. 4.42
STEINOVITZ Jacob	28.439	7. 7.04	5. 5.42	WALD Simon	28.021	1. 3.21	1. 7.42
STERN Berthold	27.652	14. 2.00	2. 5.42	WARHTER Nachman	28.087	.03	23. 4.42
STERN Jacob	27.648	22. 6.97	21. 4.42	WASNTRAVB Israël	28.639	27. 6.96	8. 5.42
STERNBERG Samuel	28.355	19.10.08	7. 5.42	WASSERSTEIN Bernard	27.762	24.12.99	7. 7.42
STRAZ Naftula	27.823	23. 7.02	21. 4.42	WAWER Abraham	27.779	16.11.97	7. 5.42
STRUMFELD Missislaw	28.561	13. 6.19	18. 6.42	WEICHLEDER Enia	28.329	17. 8.96	14. 6.42
STRYNESKI Émile	28.276	1. 3.20	24. 4.42	WEIL Andréas	27.654	5. 6.04	1. 7.42
SUSSHOLZ Mayer	27.969	31. 1.97	8. 5.42	WEILL Karl	27.881	27. 1.21	23. 4.42
SWIADOCHT Georges	27.937	12. 6.91	15. 4.42	WEINBERG Chem	27.677	23. 1.98	24. 4.42
SWIRMANN Émile	27.606	9. 9.99	13. 6.42	WEISS Otto	27.833	10. 1.18	2. 6.42
SYCH Mayer	28.417	20.12.98	26. 5.42	WEISSER Max	28.176	1. 4.14	7. 5.42

Adolph's Auschwitz number and date of his death

conversation which a section leader (SS man) conducted with the section elder, who was a German inmate. One day, the section leader asked the section elder how many corpses there were. The section elder answered him that today he had 35 corpses in his block and the section leader declared: "That is good." In each sec-

---

Waschkiewicz   Annex

Waschkiewicz, Wladislawa (-.-.1926,
 Lawsko, 10.6.1943) — HbZl 2 (569,570)
Waschkiewicz, Wladislawa (-.-.1931,
 Lomza, 10.6.1943) — HbZl 2 (567,568)
Wasiela, Jozef (16.2.1895, Pludwiny,
 31.3.1943) — StUrk. 4 (8)
Wasilewski, Siegmund (7.4.1904, —,
 28.4.1942) — Stb. 1 (288-292)
Wasilewski, Zbigniew (4.9.1910, —,
 20.6.1942) — Stb. 2 (17-18)
Wasilkowic, Helene (-.-.1940, Stahlberg,
 19.1.1944) — HbZl 1 (49,50)
Waskowski, Helene (5.9.1943, Birkenau
 b.Auschwitz, 11.5.1944) — HbZl 2
 (609,610)
Wasowicz, Johann (26.3.1910, —, 15.6.1942)
 — Stb. 1 (542-546)
Wasser, Max Israel (1.4.1914, —, 7.5.1942)
 — Stb. 1 (324-329)
Wassermann, Rojzal Sara (8.9.1906, —,
 8.12.1943) — Stv. 16 (54-63)
Wastian, Stefan (8.10.1905, —, 29.5.1944) —
 BdSk. 1 (39)
Wasylkowitsch, Johann (-.-.1937, Limburg,
 6.1.1944) — HbZl 1 (116)
Waterman, Anna Sara (16.7.1919, —,
 7.12.1943) — Stv. 16 (45-53)
Watermann, Betty Sara (26.3.1916, —,
 6.12.1943) — Stv. 16 (35-44)
Wawer, Abraham Israel (16.11.1897, —,
 7.5.1942) — Stb. 1 (324-329)
Wawro, Boleslaus (9.3.1901, —, 24.7.1942)
 — Stb. 2 (200-206)
Wawro, Johann (15.12.1897, —, 23.4.1942)
 — Stb. 1 (271-274)
Wawrzen, Konstanty (11.9.1903,
 Przemeczany, 9.2.1944) — StUrk. 4 (32)
Wayntraub, Israel (27.6.1896, —, 3.5.1942)
 — Stb. 1 (307-308)
Wdowka, Leo (28.6.1907, —, 15.6.1942) —
 Stb. 1 (546-549)
Weber, Blima Sara (24.12.1924, —,
 6.12.1943) — Stv. 16 (35-44)
Weber, Miriam Sara (18.2.1915, —,
 6.12.1943) — Stv. 16 (35-44)
Weber, Paula Sara (29.7.1913, —, 8.12.1943)
 — Stv. 16 (54-63)
Wege, Otto (16.4.1890, —, 9.5.1942) —
 Stb. 1 (334-339)

Węgielek, Ladislas (5.10.1895, Warka,
 28.9.1943) — Bb. 2 (44)
Weichleder, Elia (17.8.1896, —, 14.6.1942)
 — Stb. 1 (539-541)
Weichrauch, Margot (11.1.1927, Berlin,
 4.6.1944) — HbZl 1 (263,264)
Weichrauch, Sonia (6.9.1929, Berlin,
 4.2.1944) — HbZl 1 (261,262)
Weider, Josef (31.5.1937, Wien, -.-.1944) —
 HbZl 1 (207)
Weidlaowicz, Wawnymich (-.-.1928,
 Miczibowo, 2.6.1943) — HbZl 1 (239)
Weidmann, Ignats (28.8.1913, Humenne,
 16.6.1942) — Zl. 1 (8); Stb. 1 (556-560)
Weifs, Eugen (8.2.1932, Metz, -.-.1944) —
 HbZl 1 (274)
Weigl, Moritz Isr. (6.2.1860, —, 7.1.1944) —
 Stv. 16 (70-72)
Weihrauch, Johann (21.6.1902, Porne,
 -.-.1943) — HbZl 1 (91)
Weil, Alfred Isr. (8.9.1866, —, 7.1.1944) —
 Stv. 16 (70-72)
Weil, Andreas (5.6.1904, —, 1.5.1942) —
 Stb. 1 (300-303)
Weil, Filip Israel (26.7.1885, —, 18.8.1942)
 — Stb. 2 (364-372)
Weil, Josef (30.4.1895, Turcansky Svaty
 Martin, 3.5.1942) — Zl. 1 (37); Stb. 1
 (308-311)
Weill, Madeleine Sara (13.3.1905, —,
 6.12.1943) — Stv. 16 (35-44)
Weill, Roger (22.3.1904, —, 11.6.1942) —
 Stb. 1 (525-527)
Wein, Josef (23.3.1925, —, 7.5.1942) —
 Stb. 1 (324-329)
Weinberg, Fanny Sara (7.10.1905, —,
 7.12.1943) — Stv. 16 (45-53)
Weinberg, Schmul Isr. (23.2.1902, Dziewiek,
 22.5.1943) — Bb. 2 (8)
Weinberger, Adalbert (5.10.1887,
 Kenderesz, 5.5.1942) — Zl. 1 (34); Stb. 1
 (320-322)
Weinberger, Eisig (10.10.1912, —,
 19.6.1942) — Stb. 2 (7-10); MEvZ 2
 (626)
Weinberger, Emanuel (13.3.1901,
 Michalovce, 19.6.1942) — Zl. 1 (9);
 Stb. 2 (13-16)

1632

Adolph's death as recorded in the Auschwitz Death Book

tion, there was a SS man who was section leader, the section elder was a German inmate, his representative was a Pole and the indoor workers were Jews. The system of government in each block was designed so that the section leader forced the section elder to torment and harrass the inmates. He then forced his representative, who then forced his representative, who forced his representative who along those lines tormented and harrassed the indoor workers. As a consequence, the indoor workers did everything at the cost of the inmates to gain a good reputation. Under conditions like this, I spent five weeks at Birkenau. [258]

Adolph lived for five weeks at Auschwitz. The horrible day-to-day accounts of the terrible events are well-documented. [259] I was fortunate to acquire his Auschwitz number, 28176, and his official date of death, May 7, 1942. [260] His name also appears in the Auschwitz Death Books. Under his name, there is the abbreviation, Stb 1. a reference to the Starkebuch or daybook. All the entries included the following: "entry number, prisoner category, prisoner number, last and first names and date of birth. The entries indicated the total at the time of the morning and evening roll calls." [261] The last entry in the daybook was the date of death, which was based on a "death report issued by the sick bay." [262]The death report included prisoners who had been shot or killed by phenol injections or other means. [263] Adolph was one of "156 persons who died in May from Convoy 1. During the first five months, 91 per cent of the people on the first convoy died. "[264] Adolph wanted what many people want, a full long life, to work, to socialize and to maintain ties to his family. That was all cut short at the age of 28. Auschwitz replaced all his hopes and dreams with a nightmare existence. For those five weeks, he had the added burden of his physical handicap, which must have made his life there all the more unbearable.

The family knew he was deported to Auschwitz, but did not know the date of his death. In spite of numerous inquiries, the Red Cross refused to provide them with any information on him.

The family was very much concerned about Albert, who was still in prison at Avignon. Fortunately, police officials who were members of the resistance movement and who were well-aware of Albert's involvement, would delay his case from coming to trial by putting his case on the bottom of the pile of other pending cases.

They left Paris shortly before the massive rounds, "Les Rafles" of July 1942. They probably left Paris before June 18, 1942 because at that time there was a massive raid on Menilmontant. [265] The date of departure was after June 7th, because it was at that time, Mina remembers picking up the Jewish star, which was mandated to be worn by all Jews. She picked it up, but never wore it.

The wearing of the star was intended to make the Jews a visible target and to humiliate them. It also meant other actions were forthcoming. These thoughts were utmost in the minds of family members, and explains why no one from the family ever wore the Jewish star.

Like so many other Parisian Jews, they had to register with the Police. Family members gave no thought to this demand but it was an important step in the identification and concentration of the Jews. At the time, they were unaware of the events that represented steps toward the final solution.

The family left Paris for Avignon to be closer to Albert, who was then in prison. They undertook the perilous journey from occupied France to unoccupied France. The only way to get to the Free Zone was

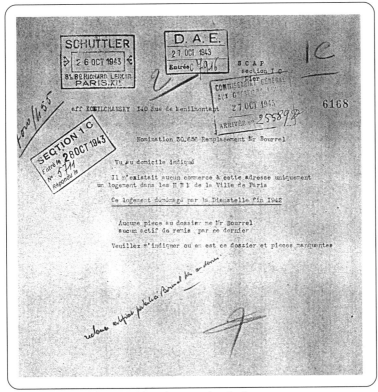

Documentation of the ransacking of my grandmother's apartment

to employ the services of passeurs who would assist escapees past German posts. Jews caught travelling to the Free Zone by these illegal means faced the risk of being interned or executed. It was not uncommon for passeurs to accept money from escapees and turn them over to the Germans.

The journey was made with the family hiding underneath the boards of a cattle train with other Jews. Before the train crossed into unoccupied France, the train stopped and they could hear the footsteps of German officers and soldiers above their heads. The atmosphere was filled with fear and apprehension. They didn't know if the passeurs would give them away or help them escape to the unoccupied zone. They knew they were willing to take an enormous risk in order to reach the unoccupied zone.

Their departure from Paris to Avignon was well-timed. A document dated October 26, 1943, provided important information on what happened to the apartment and its contents after the family left Paris. The document made reference to : "Ce logement demanage par la Dienstelle fin 1942." This reference is important for many reasons. It means that their apartment containing furniture and household items was seized by the Nazis at the end of 1942.

This document supports the testimony of my mother as to what happened to their apartment after they fled Paris. Dienstelle is short for Dienstelle Western of the Einsatzstab Rosenberg, responsible for seizures of furniture in France and other occupied countries. Furniture from vacant Jewish apartments was seized by the Dienstelle. "Of the 71,619 Jewish apartments seized, 38,000 of them were in Paris." [266] The typical procedure was

> to crate all this furniture for shipment to Germany, the office drew upon Paris shippers, who made available daily up to 150 vans and 1,200 to 1,500 French workers. However, 'sabotage' on the part of the French personnel was so great that the Einsatzstab hit upon the idea of employing 700 Jews for the sorting, packing and loading operations.[267]

Prisoners from Drancy were used to sort out the items. They were housed in one of the largest, well-known furniture stores in Paris, at that time Les Meubles Levitain. They were responsible for separating and putting into crates for shipment to Germany a range of items taken from Jewish apartments, such as furniture, clothing, linens, books, children's toys and food. My grandmother was told by a neighbor that the Germans came to their apartment at 140 Menilmontant. There were family pictures on the wall. One German threw the pictures on the floor, shattered the glass and frame with his boot and shouted in German, 'Dirty Jews!' Once the Germans had seized the furniture, many of these so-called neighbors helped themselves to the items left behind. In a final twisted message, she was told of a sign on the truck, that took away the family's possessions, it read "Gift from the French to the German people." The crates shipped to Germany upon arrival were placed on exposition for Germans to take what they chose without payment.

Had the family members remained in Paris, they would have been rounded up and deported to Auschwitz the following month. The document of July 13, 1942 leaves no doubt as to the planning and capture of

Plans of the French Police to roundup French Jews, July 1942 (xx-14a of the Archives du Centre de Documentation Juive, Paris)

■ ▮ ▮

E - Matériel :

La Compagnie du Métropolitain, réseau de surface, enverra directement les 16 et 17 Juillet à 5 heures aux Centraux d'Arrondissement où ils resteront à votre disposition jusqu'à fin de service :

- Ier Arrdt : I autobus
- 2ème   -   : I   -
- 3ème   -   : 3   -
- 4ème   -   : 3   -
- 5ème   -   : I   -
- 6ème   -   : I   -
- 7ème   -   : I   -
- 8ème   -   : I   -
- 9ème   -   : 2.   -
-10ème   -   : 3   -
-11ème   -   : 7   -
-12ème   -   : 2   -
-13ème   -   : I   -
-14ème   -   : I   -
-15ème   -   : I   -
-16ème   -   : I   -
-17ème   -   : I   -
-18ème   -   : 3   -
-19ème   -   : 3   -
-20ème   -   : 7   -

A la Préfecture de Police (Caserne de la Cité) :

6 autobus.

Lorsque vous n'aurez plus besoin des autobus, vous en aviserez d'urgence l'Etat-Major P.M., et, de toute façon vous ne les renverrez qu'avec son accord.

En outre la Direction des Services Techniques tiendra à la disposition de l'Etat-Major de ma Direction, au garage, à partir du 16 Juillet à 8 heures :

10 grands cars.

Les Arrondissements conserveront jusqu'à nouvel ordre les voiturettes mises à leur disposition pour le service spécial du 14 Juillet, contrairement aux instructions de ma Circulaire n° 170-42 du 13 Juillet.

De plus, de 6 heures à 18 heures, les 16 et 17 Juillet, un motocycliste sera mis à la disposition de chacun des : 9ème - 10ème - XIème - 18ème - 19ème et 20ème Arrdts.

F - Garde du Vélodrôme d'Hiver :

La garde du Vélodrôme d'Hiver sera assurée, tant à

....../

Jews in the 20e and the rest of Paris. [268] The 20e and 11e had the highest concentration of Jews in Paris. In many streets in the 20e, Jews were rounded up in the 'Grande Rafle.' In the Belleville section, the testimony of Jacques Zilber is witness to the roundup of Jews:

> Puis est survenue la grande rafle de Julliet 42. J'ai vu defiler tous les amis, adultes et enfants, boduchons sur les dos ou valises a la main, en tout une quinzaine de personnes...On ni retait pas venue nous chercher car nous etions de natinalite francaise et aussi peut-etre parce qu'on a eu de la chance. Nous etions caches derriere les rideaux et nous regardions sans comprendre bien et surtout sans savoid le sort qui leur etait reserve. Un soeurs (Blanche ou Ida) protestait car elle voulait 'partir en vacances' avec les copines... [269]

Another chilling account is provided by the testimony of Marcel Rozenthal in his statement, entitled, "la nuit et les Brouillard s'abbatirent sur Belleville."

"16 Juillet: Le jour de la Grande Rafled, tres tot des voisins dont les fenetres donnaient sur la rue Bisson, virent arriver les cars de police et dans tout le voisinage, les cris et les pleurs resonnaient. Les parents de Petit Louis, mon meilleur copain, ils s'appelaient Ledous, nous previnrent et nous proposerent de nous refugier chez eux. De leur fenetre, situee a la hauteur du 2eme etage, nous vimes "embraquer" des dizaines de familles, femmes, enfants..." [270]

The departure for Avignon was well-timed. As soon as they arrived, the family moved into an apartment in Avignon on the same street as the prison. There was such a sense of urgency in the family about seeing Albert, that they immediately agreed to a mere five-minute visit proposed by a sympathetic French police officer. The officer told my grandmother that Albert was being transferred to a police station for interrogation and that he would be passing their street at a particular time. When Albert passed by, he arranged for the family's brief reunion at the apartment.

My grandmother had sold everything she owned to hire a lawyer to work on Albert's case, remarking, "My son is worth everything." In Avignon, he was imprisoned with common criminals. After a period of time, he was transferred to Marseilles as a political prisoner. By this time, the Germans had crossed the free zone and occupied what had been called free France. The Germans proposed a blanket amnesty to all political prisoners. My uncle was very suspicious, thinking, why would they be so generous and let us go? So while the other prisoners went through the main door, he went out the door the lawyers use. It saved his life, because the other prisoners were led to trucks and were deported.

Having learned of Albert's escape, the family left Avignon and went to Grenoble. The reason for leaving was a fear that the French police would arrest family members living in Avignon. Grenoble, at thtat time, was under Italian occupation. According to my mother, the Italians didn't do anything to the Jews. No wonder the family moved to Grenoble. In the Italian zone, arrests of Jews were halted and those captured were released. In addition, the Italians prevented the introduction of the following measures: "They refused to allow foreign labor camps in their occupation zone. They forbade the word 'Jew' as required by a recent French law. In March, they ordered the French government to annul all arrests and internments of Jews in their zone, including French Jews." [271]

My mother at age 17

My mother and her twin sister, Grenoble 1942

There were also a lot of Italians living in Grenoble. Italian soldiers made friends with families living there. While living in Grenoble, members of the family maintained contact with members of the French underground and very often the house was used for a drop and for meetings.

My mother had false papers from the Prefecture de Police as did everyone in the family. She went by the name Aline Robert. Everyone knew my grandfather as Mr. Robert. Of equal importance to changing one's name was changing one's date of birth. If you were over 17 or 18, you would be subject to forced labor. My mother's place of birth also was changed to Madagascar. My grandmother had to say she was born in Switzerland because she had an accent, so she couldn't be French.

The first time my mother used her false papers, they were in a village near Grenoble, Ste. Nizier des Moucherottes, in the restaurant of a hotel. My mother and my aunt were sitting in a restaurant after skiing. My mother remembers hearing shots and returned gunfire. A member of the FTP had wounded two German soliders and killed another. His fellow Resistance members in the car tried to escape but the car would not start. They tried to escape on foot. What followed 2-3 hours later was the arrival en masse of German soldiers and officers. My mother remembers the door being kicked open by Germans with machine guns drawn. She remembers clearly two members of the Gestapo who arrived wearing the typical long leather coats and black boots. They came in front of the tables and asked for papers. Men were segregated from women. Some

Robert and Dora Kolnitchanski with Albert (back), 1943

of the men were killed with rifle butts in the stomach while looking straight in the eyes of the perpetrators. The Gestapo said to the women assembled, "You know who the terrorists are." Nothing was said.

My mother remembers her heart was pounding because she feared being discovered. On another occasion, she was walking in the street when suddenly, all the entranceways to the street were blocked. It was like being caught in a trap, she said. The Germans yelled "Papers! Papers!" A German soldier looked at my mother's false identity card. She was terrified, not knowing what the consequences would be, but he let her go to her great relief.

After Albert's escape, he visited the family. It was the last time he would see his father alive. Albert went then to the French Alps and once again, was actively working in the French underground. After the liberation of France, he went to Italy and fought during the Italian campaign. Then he was sent to Austria to serve in the Alpine troops as part of the French Army. The Austrians were petrified of the Alpine troops whose blue uniform and big beret made them think they were members of a French SS. Both my mother and aunt conveyed the sense that the Austrians were petrified of Albert. He was particularly hard in his treatment of prisoners, given the fact that he knew full well that his father had been deported just six months before. It was common practice for members of these units to stay in the homes of Austrians. Uncle Albert stayed in the home of a notable, who tried to be friendly and hospitable, making references to two products of German culture, Bach and Beethoven. In response, Albert angrily replied, "Why do you speak of Bach and Beethoven? Speak of Auschwitz and Matterhausen."

By the end of the war, Albert had received three medals, de la resistance, de l'Armee, Chausseurs d'Alpine.

PREMIER MINISTRE

MINISTÈRE
DES ANCIENS COMBATTANTS
ET VICTIMES DE GUERRE
37, RUE DE BELLECHASSE - 75700 PARIS 07 SP
TÉL. (1) 44.42.10.00

RÉPUBLIQUE FRANÇAISE

Paris, le   **14 NOV 1996**

N°   ᴣ६१९   EC-1/JC/OD
Affaire suivie par :
M. Jean Canitrot
Tél. : 44.42.16.91

DELEGATION A LA MEMOIRE
ET A L'INFORMATION HISTORIQUE
Département du patrimoine
Section Etat civil

Monsieur,

Vous avez bien voulu me demander des renseignements sur deux de vos parents.

J'ai l'honneur de vous faire connaître, après consultation du dossier en ma possession, que votre grand-père, Monsieur Ruben KOLNITCHANSKI, né le 15 septembre 1883 à POVONZNOWSKI (Russie) était de nationalité française (naturalisé par décret du 16 novembre 1913).

Il était domicilié 14, rue de Ménilmontant à PARIS 20ème, mais demeurait 2, rue des Iles à GRENOBLE (Isère) au moment de son arrestation.

Suivant un témoignage, Monsieur KOLNITCHANSKI a été arrêté le 15 janvier 1944 en gare de GRENOBLE, par mesure de représaille, à la suite de la découverte dans un train venant de CHAMBERY de munitions dissimulées par la Résistance. Interné d'abord à CHAMBERY, puis transféré le 19 janvier 1944 à DRANCY, il a été déporté le 3 février 1944 au camp de concentration d'AUSCHWITZ où il est décédé le 8 février 1944.

Son acte de décès a été dressé par mes services le 22 mars 1944 et transcrit le 27 juin 1947 sur les registres de la mairie du 20ème arrondissement à PARIS (registre 392, acte n° 1955) à laquelle vous devrez vous adresser pour obtenir une expédition. Par ailleurs, la mention "Mort pour la France" a été portée en marge de l'acte de décès de Monsieur KOLNITCHANSKY et le titre de déporté politique lui a été attribué par décision du 5 août 1954.

Document from Ministere des Anciens Combattants et Victims de Guerre. My grandfather was caught in a roundup of suspected members of the French Resistance who were smuggling weapons on a train bound for Chamberry

Mina saw her father for the last time on January 14, 1944. At the time, she wanted to go with him to the railroad station. He said to her, "go home it's cold," and he told her to get some coffee. The last memory Mina has of him is him turning around and waving goodbye. He was on his way to Lyon. At the station, a roundup was underway for the train going to Lyon. From the Ministere des Anciens Combattants,[272] , I received some important details as to the circumstances of his arest. In part, what this document revealed was that the Nazis had prior knowl-

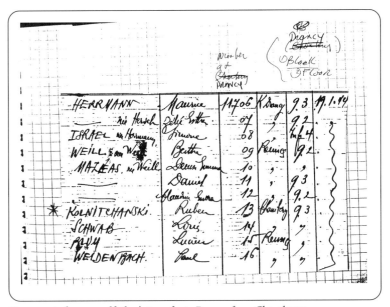

Document of my grandfather's transfer to Drancy from Chamberry

edge of a train arriving with weapons for the French resistance.

From other witnesses, the family learned about other details and about Robert's efforts to inform them of what happened. They were told that he threw his ration card on the floor of the train station with the hope, which later was realized, that the card would be mailed to the family. A railroad worker sent my grandfather's ration card back to the family. A telegram was sent by the family to know if he had arrived in Lyon, they were concerned because whenever he traveled, he would write a letter and send it to them. When the family did not hear from him, they knew right away something was wrong. News spread fast that a roundup had taken place in the Grenoble train station.

The family inquired as to his whereabouts at the Red Cross. No information was forthcoming, since he was Jewish and the Germans never gave information on the Jews to the Red Cross.

He spent about four days in Chanberry before he was transferred to Drancy, a half-completed apartment complex in a suburb of Paris. It was an antechamber to Auschwitz. As a transit camp, its primary function was to transport large numbers of Jews to Poland, where most were killed. "All but twelve of the seventy-nine deportation trains carrying Jews to the east left from Drancy." [273] My grandfather was confined there for fifteen days from January 19 to February 3, 1944[274] in one of the large dor-

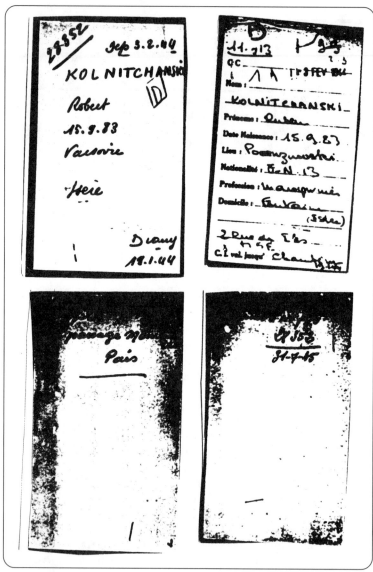

Drancy registration cards for my grandfather, French National Archives

mitories, where prisoners spent all day every day, except for a one and a half hour walk in the compound. Drancy served its intended purpose to isolate the prisoners from the outside world, starting with the use of triple walls in the form of a circle around the camp. This sense of isolation was further compounded by the fact that very few prisoners received packages or letters. In addition, prisoners were not allowed to meet in groups. These were some of the conditions my grandfather had to endure. One of the most difficult problems he and other prisoners faced was the overall lack of hygiene. Lice and fleas were everywhere. The toilet facilities were completely inadequate, with only 60 toilets for 3,000 people and the lack of toilet paper, for the most part, contributed to the spread of disease. Bathing was only allowed once every two weeks. [275]

In addition to the Ministere des Anciens Combattants, other archival material confirms what happened to Robert Kolnitchanski. From the index file of Drancy, two cards summarize his terrible fate.

My grandfather's death notice

On one card, in the top left hand corner is Robert's number at Drancy. From the top to the bottom of the card is his name, date of birth, nationality, profession and last addresses in Grenoble. At the top right hand side is the date February 3, 1944. That date also appears at the top right hand side of the second card. On the bottom of the card is the date of Jan. 19, 1944, when he transferred to Drancy from Chanberry. The D next to his name meant that he was to be deported. It was some time after the war that the family learned from someone at Drancy, who was interned with him, that he gave a French policeman a solid gold watch to mail a letter to the family. The letter was never mailed.

I will never know if my grandfather survived the five-day nightmare of travel to arrive at Auschwitz. Conditions were such in the transport to ensure a high mortality rate. Extreme overcrowding of each wagon produced an horrific mixture of living and dead bodies: "In the wagon (originally for 40 men and 8 horses) 80 were packed in. Dead bodies start to pile up, and we threw the bodies back and forth against each other — to defend our place in the wagon." [276]

The Jews in the transports were on their way to a certain death, the Nazi perpetrators created the conditions in each wagon so that the victims were dehumanized along the way. "In the dawn of the third day, more dead, thirst tortures us. The pail of urine spills a few times and the stink is suffocating. Some of us become mad, scream and violence erupts." [277]

If my grandfather lived through these conditions, he and the survivors were processed in Auschwitz, according to the set procedures in which the victims were fed into an assembly line of death.

> The train slows down, someone near the window of the wagon looks out to see snow all over and rails. I (Holt) see shadows and silhouettes, they are running, there are SS and dogs. Outside one hears voices, shouting, metal sounds of doors unlocking. The door opens suddenly blinding us by the light from the outside and subjected to freezing cold. Before we can react, we are thrown out of the wagon and piled up in the snow and mud. The other half of us are piled up on the floor of the wagon, they will never move again.
>
> The beating starts, given by people wearing big grey and blue stripes. They look like convicts. They seem to have only one thought in mind, it is to push us towards a tall SS officer who with a brief gesture directs us to the right or to the left. Our wagon was in front, behind us in 15 other wagons the same scene was repeated. [278]

In an official document, Robert Kolnitchanski, in spite of the reference to Auschwitz, is declared "Mort Pour la France." This represents a failure to acknowledge that the deportations to Auschwitz were in large part the end result of Nazi efforts to exterminate the Jews. The French government instead identified the deaths as political and not group murders. At the time of his arrival at Auschwitz, the camp had evolved into an assembly line of death. "With an average of 6,000 arrivals in Auschwitz during January through April 1944."[279] If he had survived the ordeal to reach Auschwitz, he would have been murdered in either Crematoria II or III, where "...approximately three quarters of the Jewish victims of KL Auschwitz Birkenau were gassed and reduced to ashes in these two buildings."[280] Without word from her husband, Dora thought it wise to take her children and move to a small town. They returned to Grenoble sometime after June 6, 1944. Once news had spread of the liberation of Grenoble, they took a trolley to return to the city.

As the allied armies advanced toward Paris, the 20th Arrondissement like so many other arrondissements was organizing to retake the capital from the remaining Germans.

Many acts of resistance and attacks were made on the Germans in the 20e. Some of these actions occured in my mother's street, Menilmontant. One attack by the resistance took place on August 20th: "Le 20 aout une groupe de la milice patriotique sous la direction de Jean (Tancerman) fit sauter un train plein de soldats allemands sous le pont de Menilmontant. Les militaires allemands restes in vie ont ete faits prisonniers."[281]

Another act of resistance also took place in Menilmontant on August 23, 1944:

> Le 22 aout 1944, au matin un train ennemi est longtemps immobilise en gare de Charonne. Un wagon renverse sur la voie l'empeche de passer. La voie une fois degagee, il file sur Menilmontant ou il arrive vers neuf heures. Mais il ne peut poursuivre sa route: un autre train ennemi est sur la voie en sense inverse. Le passage est bloque pourtous deux. C'est une 'erreur d'aiguillage' des cheninots...Pour les FFI, FTP, milices patriotiques du 20eme, qui occupait le pont de Menilmontant au dessus de la voie, c'est le signal de l'attaque.[282]

In and around the 20e, acts of resistance were frequent on many streets. "Rue de la Justice, le 23 aout, un convoi est attaque par les FTP..."[283] "Rue d'Avron, une certaine d'Allemands sont attaques par des FFI. . ."[284]

Besides violent encounters, resistance in the 20e took other forms, such as strikes and demonstrations. For example in July 14, in Belleville, "A 18 heures, rue de Belleville, s'est deroulee une manifestation tres importante."[285] The same day, a demonstration unfolded in rue de Menilmontant. "Rue de Menilmontant (coin rue des Amandiers) a midi tapant, la manifestation commerce."[286]

My mother, still in Grenoble, was unaware of all this resistance activity in her neighborhood. She returned with her sister and mother to

140 rue Menilmontant to find another family living in their apartment, so they were provided with another place to live.

After everything they did to survive and the loss of a husband and son, my grandmother was asked by the owner of a grocery story where they frequently shopped, "You're back?" Anti-Semitism was alive and well in post-war Paris. My mother and her sister were fortunate to have survived and not been caught, because as twins, they would have ended up in the hands of Mengele at Auschwitz.

My mother's comments about what was thought about those who did survive the camps are quite revealing as to the early post-war response regarding survivors. As news of the Holocaust began to disseminate, with all the horrors of the camps, the thinking, she said, was that to survive the camps, one must have worked for the Germans. At first, she thought of these survivors as servants of the Germans. It was not long after, as additional information circulated in Paris that she changed her opinion of them.

It was also after the war that the family learned of the murder of Dora's parents at Auschwitz. They were hiding in Paris and had come out of hiding to return to their apartment in order to celebrate the Passover seder. A neighbor informed the Gestapo and they were arrested. Like so many other Jews deported to Auschwitz, they were incarcerated in Drancy.

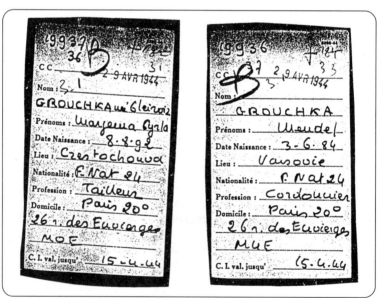

Dora Kolnitchanski's parents Drancy cards

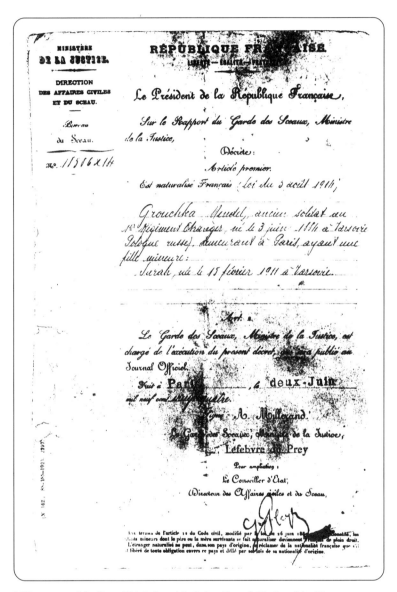

Military record for Dora Kolnitchanski's father, French National Archives

Mendel Grouchka

Their registration cards contained relevant information, such as their numbers (19936 and 7), their dates and places of birth, naturalization, occupations and their last address in Paris. [287] Their police files contain the chilling references to Jewish dossiers with the number 55521. Their deportations are one example of the Nazi's intent to exterminate the Jews until the very end. Mendel Grouchka had arrived in Paris one year earlier, before the start of WWI. He joined the French Army and served during the war in the first foreign regiment. My grandmother's parents were deported on Convoy 72, April 29, 1944,[288] about four months before Free French forces under Charles DeGaulle liberated Paris.

NOTES

[231]Paul Webster, <u>Petain's Crime</u> (Chicago: Ivan Dee, 1991) p. 30

[232]Jacques Adler, <u>The Jews of Paris and the Final Solution</u> (New York: Oxford Press, 1987) p. 8

[233]The figures of the arrondissement census are in Adler, p. 10.

[234]Jeremy Joseph, <u>Swastika over Paris: Fate of the French Jews</u>, Great Britain: Bloomsbury, 1989, p. 16

[235]Le XXe 1939-1945 souffre, il reste et se libere, section A

[236]Gerold Walter, <u>Paris under the Occupation</u>, New York: Orion Press, 1960 p. 20

[237]The references in the text are to AJ[38] 1832 dossier 17000/455

[238] Richard Weisberg,<u> Vichy Law and the Holocaust in France</u>, New York: New York University Press, 1996 p. 281

[239]Weisberg, p. 335

[240]Michael Maurus and Robert Paxton <u>Vichy France and the Jews </u>(New York: Shocken Books, 1981) p. 7

[241]Ibid, p. 129

[242]Ibid, p. 153

[243]Ibid, p. 129

[244]Webster, p. 143

[245]Ibid.

[246]Jacques Ravine <u>Le Resistance Organise des Juifs en France</u> <u>1940-44</u> (Paris: Julliard, 1973) p. 67

[247]Walter, p. 171

248Ibid.

[249] Adam Rutkowski, "Le Camp Royallieu a Compiegne"<u>, Le Monde Juif</u>, Paris: 1981, p. 125

[250]Adolph's legal status at the time of his arrest was as a foreign or stateless Jew. Evidence of this appears in immigration and naturalization files on the Kolnitchanski family. Adolph's status was defined in relation to a 1938 law:
6)Un courrier en date du 09 mai 1952:
Par une demande a propos de Wasser (Abraham Calka) pour lequel sa mere Graucke (Dwojra), epouse Kolnitchanski demeurant a Paris 140, rue de Menilmontant a suscite la delivrance d'un certificat de nationalite francaise;
Il resulte du dossier, 1)que le sus nomme est ne a Varsovie (Pologne) le 1er avril 1914. 2) Que sa mere devenue veuve S'est remariee en 1920 avec un sieur Kolnitchanski (francais par naturalisation) alors qui'il etait encore mineur et a

176 One Family: Before and During the Holocaust

acquis de ce fait notre nationalite. Toutefois, dans un arret du 29 novembre 1938 la cour de cassation a decidee que l'article 12 & 3 ancien du code civil ne pourrait etre applique a l'enfant d'un premier lit dont la mere a acquis la nationalite francais par l'effet d'un mariage condamnant ainst une pratique administrative anterieur.

En consequence, Monsieur Wasser ne saurait etre considere comme ayant acquit an undroit a note nationalite.

²⁵¹Rutkowski, p. 130

²⁵²George Wellers, L'Etoile Jaune Drancy a Auschwitz a Heure de Vichy, Paris: Fayard, 1973, p. 106

²⁵³Rutkowski, p. 122

²⁵⁴Rutkowski, pp. 141-142

²⁵⁵Paxton, p. 227

²⁵⁶Paxton, p. 226

²⁵⁷Serge Klarsfeld, Memorial to the Jews Deported from France 1922-1944 New York: Beate Klarsfeld Foundation 1983 p. 16

²⁵⁸Stanislaw Jankowski's statement appears in Inmitten Des Grauenvollen Verbrechens (Poland: Auschwitz-State Museum, 1996) pp.25-27

²⁵⁹Danuta Czech, Auschwitz Chronicle 1939-1945 (London: I.V. Tauris, 1990) pp.151-163

²⁶⁰I am grateful for the assistance of another French aunt, Marthe Weissberg. She is well-known in Paris for her work at Centre de Documentation Juive Contemporaine. She was instrumental in arranging very quickly an appointment with Serge Klarsfeld. He provided me with the document on Adolph.

²⁶¹Death Books from Auschwitz, (London: K.G. Saur, 1995) p. 37

²⁶²Ibid.

²⁶³Ibid, p. 1632

From the statements of relatives and an archival source, I learned the fate of another Kolniczanski who perished in Auschwitz. His name appears in the Auschwitz Death Books (London: 1995) p. 599 as Heinrich Kolnitzansky. The registration number 1737 and location — Warsaw — where he was caught provided clues as to how he ended up in Auschwitz. The evidence appears in Wactaw Bartoszewski , 1859 Days Under the German Occupation. As of August 12, 1940, there was a mass roundup in the city. A total of 1,153 people were caught and 513 prisoners from Pawiak deported to Auschwitz on August 12, 1940. This was the first transport from Warsaw to Auschwitz. The prisoners received numbers 1513 to 3179.

I have reason to believe his name was changed before his capture in order to pass as a Pole. The basis for this claim was my contact with descendants of Abram Kolniczanski, members of the Wiorek family in Sweden. Bertil Wiorek was helpful in providing a chart of his family. Heinrich Kolnitzansky's real name is Chaim Kolniczanski, the son of Mortre, who in turn, was the son of Abram. Chaim's date of birth and the date of his death at Auschwitz in the Death Book, match exactly the information on the Wiorek family chart.

Chaim suffered for three agonizing years, a lifetime in Auschwitz, since most victims could only expect to live a few months. He lived through the many phases of Auschwitz. He arrived in August, just after Himmler started to outline his plan for a German east in July. The plan included the Germanization of the territory around Auschwitz. As of September, Pohl was transforming Auschwitz into a part of an elaborate SS financial empire. Also by 1940, the small crematoriums were at work burning corpses. Chaim survived the development of Auschwitz in 1941-42 as a mass killing center. His death on January 19, 1943 was one of 53 recorded in Auschwitz on that day, according to Danuta Czech, Auschwitz Chronicle.

[264]Klarsfeld, p. 2

[265]Walter, p. 187

[266]Paxton p. 129

[267]Raul Hilberg, The Destruction of the European Jews Vol. V (New York: Holmes/Meier, 1985) p. 659

[268]Archives du Centre de Documentation Juive Contemporaire, document XX-14A

[269]Le XXe Soffre Resiste, se libre recits, temonoignager, documents, photos: une contribution des Communists au 5eme anniversaire de la liberation

[270]Ibid

[271]Susan Zuccotti, The Italians and the Holocaust, New York: Basic Books, 1987, pp. 83-84

[272]Ministere des Anciens Combattants et victimes de guerre, No. 3619 EC-1/JC/OD

[273]Paxton, Vichy p. 522

[274]I am once again thankful to Serge Klarsfeld for providing this document.

[275]These conditions are discussed in great detail in Maurice Rajsfus, Drancy, un camp de concentration tres ordinare 1941-1944 , (Le Vallois-Perret, Manya, 1991) pp. 170-178

[276]A recent account written by a non-Jewish survivor of Convoy 67, Willy Holt: Femmes un decil sur un camion (Paris: Nil editions, 1995) p. 19

[277]Ibid, pp. 20-21

[278]Ibid.

[279] Deborah Dwork and Robert Jan Van Pelt, Auschwitz 1270 to the Present,

(New York: W.W. Norton, 1996) p. 337

[280]Ibid.

[281]Le xxe Section D

[282]Ibid

[283]Ibid

[284]Ibid

[285]Ibid

[286]Ibid

[287]National Archives, Paris, Scl919 pJ: 6

[288]Klarsfeld, p. 548

CHAPTER EIGHT

The Conclusion

F ROM START TO FINISH, my motivation to research this family amounts to an act of recovery. To restore the memory of the generational chain of this family, both how it was established and how the links of the chain were broken, is an act of recovery. For me, the key to understanding the members of this family was to identify with who they were, both prior and during the Holocaust.

In essence, recovery of a memory of this family functioned as an obligation to speak for them, allowing them to speak to a larger audience, making public how they lived and how they died. The obligation to remember them is, in a sense, fulfilled by the creation of a public record of their lives. To do the opposite, to repress the memory would be a form of additional victimization.

As a personal and professional journey, there were a number of striking impressions gathered over the course of this research. These impressions were gathered during visits to Poland and France. Visiting Poland was more than a pilgrimage; it turned out to be a country with no visible indications of a Jewish past, of Jewish life, what is visible are the signs of Jewish death. Of a pre-Holocaust past for my relatives, there were a few abstract signs of their presence, such as the names of streets where they lived and the site of the slaughterhouse. Nonetheless, the buildings are new, the slaughterhouse was torn down in 1975. There are no surviving tangible representations of where and how they lived, no living relatives to speak to. Warsaw symbolized the destruction of this family's chain of being. What remains are the horrifying symbols of their deaths. Warsaw, Poland was a place where I could not search for roots, instead it was a place where the roots had been ripped out; in their place, are grave sites. The memorial messages in Warsaw, as well as in Auschwitz and Majdanek, were mixed, some conveyed a message that the victims were Jewish, others conveyed that victims were Polish.

I was struck by the contradiction between the Umschagplatz monument in Warsaw and Auschwitz. While the Umschagplatz emphasizes the Jewish victims, the camps where they arrived did not stress the victims as Jewish but Polish. The set-up of Auschwitz as a memorial emphasizes Auschwitz I and not Birkenau.

> The main camp first and foremost, preserved Polish, not Jewish history, however, and the decision to relegate Birkenau to a position of secondary importance reflects a specific ideology of remembrance.[281]

My associations of where relatives were murdered are not with Auschwitz I, but Birkenau.

Auschwitz I, as it is today, has a reception center located adjacent to the parking lot; it houses a restaurant, cafeteria, post office, book shop and hotel. In 1942, when my mother's brother Max Wasser arrived in Auschwitz, this building was the reception center for prisoners, where they

> passed through a series of large rooms, each designated for a specific function. First they were registered and tattooed, then they surrendered their valuables and finally they were forced to undress. Their garments were taken to the delousing units while they went in a different direction to be shaved. The gas chambers for the clothing were parallel to the shower room for the inmates — a juxtaposition that was to merge into a single lethal construct in Birkenau. The prisoners dried in the next room and then pushed into another where striped pyjamas were thrown at them.[282]

It was while walking in Birkenau, not Auschwitz I, that I understood and felt that this was the place where my relatives were swallowed up and murdered in what seems to the naked eye to be a vast, never-ending murder factory. The sheer size and scale of Birkenau seems to overwhelm one's ability to comprehend the planned steps involved in an industrialized form of mass murder.

In spite of the emphasis on Polish victims in the signs and explanations, which I chose to ignore, Majdanek was, for me, a contrast to

Birkenau in that I could comprehend all at once the steps taken to murder the victims. The reason had to do with the size and presentation of the camp. My thoughts in both camps were overshadowed by profound grief, which ran through every fiber of my being as I stood inside the gas chamber in Majdanek and outside the remains of Crematoria II and III in Birkenau. It was this on-site reality of the murder of relatives that served to strengthen my resolve to obligate myself to record their fate.

My understanding of French relatives took shape over many years, determined by a complex set of conditions unique to the family and France. From the point of view of researching, it was possible to sidestep the often problematic interplay between memory and history. They tended to complement each other in more or less the following terms:

> History may never capture certain elements of memory: the feel of an experience, the intensity of joy or suffering, the quality of an occurrence. Yet history also includes elements that are not exhausted by memory, such as demographic, ecological and economic factors. [283]

The blend of memory and history was possible because a large number of relatives survived; many archival documents also survived. The survival of both witnesses and records is, simply put, the fundamental difference that accounts for why the record of French relatives is more complete than that of the Polish ones.

With this difference in mind, a psychology of the French relatives can be constructed. The main element that is dominant is the implication that survival must mean an affirmation of life. Their Holocaust past did not destroy their future hopes and dreams. They moved forward, yet always in touch with their Holocaust past, talking about it, attempting to understand it. This is especially the case for my grandmother, mother, aunt and uncle.

Dora Kolnitchanski returned to work as a pocketbook seller, Aunt Mina also continued working with pocketbooks and later opened her own clothing store. Uncle Albert married, had one daughter and for many years, had a successful scrap metal business. My mother came to the U.S., married, raised two sons and worked for many years.

I conclude with a brief comment on the American branch of the family. With the exception of my grandparents, Max and Tillie, the Holocaust was a distant event without direct relevance. This is a commentary on the effects of a failure to remember. At least I can say that the post-war passing of relatives was natural, not artifical; their lives were not cut short due to the extremes of hatred taken to a murderous end.

NOTES

[281] Deborah Dwork and Robert Jan Van Pelt Reclaiming Auschwitz in Holocaust Remembrance, ed. by Geoffrey Hartman Oxford University Press 1995, p. 241

[282] Ibid, pp. 237-238

[283] Dominick LaCapra History and Memory After Auschwitz, Cornell Press, Ithaca, 1998 p. 20

Sources

ARCHIVES

National Archives, Stockholm, Sweden

State Archive, Archangel, Russia

National Archives, Copenhagen, Denmark

Archives, U.S. Department of Immigration

National Archive, Paris, France

Prefecture de Police, Paris, France

Maries de Paris, Direction des Parcs et Espaces Verts, Service Des Cimetieres, Cimetiere de Bagneux

Archive, Hebrew Butcher's Union, Local 342-50 New York

Jewish Historical Institute, Warsaw Poland

Yad Vashem, Jerusalem Israel

Archives du Centre de Documentation Juives
    Contemporaire, Paris France

Ministere des Anciens Combattants et Victimes de Guerre, Paris France

LETTERS AND INTERVIEWS

Frydman, Adam	Australia, personal communication, letters to Andrew Kolin, 1996-1999
Galanty, Bella	New York, Interviews, Fall 1996, Spring 1997
Kolin, Helene	New York, Interviews, 1996-1998
Kolin, Morris	New York, Interviews, 1997-1998
Kolnitchanski, Mina	New York and Paris, Interviews 1996-1998
Russell, Celia	Florida, personal communication, letters 1997-1998
Spilok, Esther	Denmark, personal communication, letters 1996-1997
Zer-hen, Nuta	Israel, personal communication, letters 1997

MEMOIRS

Alexandroni, Y. (ed.) The Yizkor Book of Augustow and Vicinity (Tel Aviv: Organization of Jews of Augustow and Vicinity, 1966)

Berg, Mary <u>Warsaw Ghetto</u> (New York: L.B. Fisher, 1945)

Czechowicz and Gurman <u>Memoirs,</u> (Warsaw, Interpress, 1993)

Goldstein, Bernard <u>Twenty Years with the Jewish Labor Bund</u> (New York: Farlag Unser Tsait, 1960)

Goldstein, Bernard <u>Five Years in the Warsaw Ghetto</u> (New York: Doubleday Books, 1961)

Holt, Willy <u>Femmes un Decil sur an Camion</u> (Paris: Nil Editions 1955)

Kruk, Moshe Unpublished diary

Lazar, Chaim <u>Muranowska 7</u> (Tel Aviv: P.E.C. Press, 1966)

Lewin, Abraham <u>A Cup of Tears</u> (London: Oxford Press, 1989)

Ringelblum, Emanuel <u>Polish Jewish Relations</u> (New York: Howard Fertig, 1976)

Ringelblum, Emanuel <u>Notes from the Warsaw Ghetto</u> (New York: Schocken Books, 1958)

Seidman, Hillel <u>Warsaw Ghetto Diaries</u> (Michigan: Tarsun Press 1997)

Secondary Sources

Alder, Jacques, <u>The Jews of Paris and the Final Solution</u> (New York: Oxford Press, 1987)

Bartoszewski, Wladyslaw <u>Warsaw Death Ring</u> (Warsaw, Interpress, 1968)

Beider, Alexander <u>A Dictionary of Polish Surnames from the Kingdom of Poland</u> (New Jersey: Avotaynu, 1996)

Belsky, Joseph <u>I, the Union: The Personalized Trade Union Story of the Hebrew Butcher's Union</u> (New York: Raddock Brothers, 1952)

Bludnikow, Bemt <u>Eastern European Jews in Copenhagen, 1904- 1920</u> (Copenhagen: Industry Press, 1986)

Blobaum, Robert <u>Revolucja, Russian Poland 1904-1907</u> (Ithaca: Cornell University Press, 1995)

Czech, Danuta <u>Auschwitz Chronicles 1939-1945</u> (London: .V. Tauris, 1990)

Dantner, Szymon, Gumkowski, Janusz, Leszcynski, Kazimierz <u>Genocide 1939-1945</u> (Warsaw: Interpress, 1962)

Davies, Norman <u>A History of Poland</u> (New York: Columbia University Press, 1982)

Desind, Philip <u>Jewish and Russian Revolutionaries Exiled to Siberia 1901-1914</u> (United Kingdom: Edwin Mellen Press, 1990)

Dobroszcki, Lucjan and Gimblett-Kirshenblatt, Barbara Image Before My Eyes: A Photographic History of Jewish Life in Poland Before the Holocaust (New York: Schocken Books, 1977)

Dwork, Deborah and PeltVan, Jan Robert Auschwitz 1270 to the Present (New York: W.W. Norton, 1996)

Ellis, John Eye Deep in Hell (Baltimore: John Hopkins Press, 1976)

Fuks, Marian Zydzi w Warsazwie (Poznan: Daszewice, 1992)

Gieysztoz, Aleksandr and Kienicwicz A History of Poland (Warsaw: Polish Scientific Publishers, 1979)

Gottlieb, Roger Thinking the Unthinkable (New York: Paulist Press, 1990)

Gutman, Yisrael The Jews of Warsaw 1939-1943 (Bloomington: Indiana University Press, 1989)

Hilberg, Raul The Destruction of the European Jews (New York: Holmes/ Meier, 1985)

Hirshaut, Julien Jewish Martyrs of Pawiak (New York: Holocaust Library, 1982)

Horne, Alistair The Price of Glory: Verdun 1916 (London: Penguin Books, 1993)

Hyman, Paula From Dreyfus to Vichy: The Remaking of French Jewry 1906-1939 (New York: Columbia Press, 1979)

Jankowski, Stanislaw Testimony in Inmitten des Grauenvollen Verbrechens (Poland: Auschwitz State Museum, 1996)

Kernish, Joseph To live and Die with Honor (Jerusalem: Yad Vashem, 1986)

Klarsfeld, Serge Memorial to the Jews Departed from France 1942-1944

Kolatch, Alfred Complete Dictionary of English and Hebrew First Names (New York: Jonathan Davis Publishers, 1984)

Leszczynska, Zofia Kronika oboza na Majdanka (Lublin: Wydawnictwo Lubelskie 1980)

Luffin, John Western Front Companion, 1914-1918 (United Kingdom: Alan Sutton Publishing, 1995)

Lustiger, Arno (ed) Black Book of Polish Jewry (Germany: Syndikat Buchgeseleschaft, 1995)

Marcus, Joseph Social and Political History: Jews in Poland 1919-1939 (New York: Mouton Publishers, 1983)

Maurus, Michael and Paxton, Robert Vichy France and the Jews (New York: Schocken Books, 1981)

Miller, William Liner (United Kingdom: Wellingbrough Press, 1986)

Rajsfus, Maurice Drancy (Le Vallois-Perret: Manya, 1991)

Ravine, Jacques Le Resistance Organise des Juifs en France 1940-1944 (Paris: Julliard, 1973)

Roland, Charles Courage Under Siege: Starvation, Disease and Death in the Warsaw Ghetto (New York: Oxford Press, 1992)

Sachar, Howard A History of Jews in America (New York: Vintage Press, 1992)

Sorin, Gerald A Time for Building: The Third Migration, 1880-1920 (Baltimore: John Hopkins Press, 1992)

Summer, Ian and Embleton The French Army 1914-1918 (London: Reed Books, 1995)

Tobias, Henry The Jewish Bund in Russia (California: Stanford University Press, 1972)

Trunk, Isaish Judenrat (Lincoln: University of Nebraska Press 1996)

Walter, Gerold Paris Under the Occupation (New York: Orion Press, 1960)

Wandycz, Piotar, The Lands of Partitioned Poland, 1795-1918 (Washington: University of Washington Press, 1974)

Webster, Paul Petain's Crime (Chicago: Ivan Dee, 1991)

Weinberg, A Community on Trial: The Jews of Paris in the 1930's (Chicago: University of Chicago Press, 1984)

Weisberg, Richard Vichy Law and the Holocaust in France (New York: NYU Press, 1996)

Wellers, George L'Etoile Jaune Drancy a Auschwitz a Heure a Heure de Vichy (Paris: Fayard, 1973)

Wenger, Beth New York Jews and the Great Depression (New Haven: Yale University Press, 1996)

Zuccotti, Susan The Italians and the Holocaust (New York: Basic Books, 1987)

Index

About the Author

Andrew Kolin is an assistant professor of political science at Hilbert College in Hamburg, New York. His previous book is <u>The Ethical Foundations of Hume's Theory of Politics</u>.